Praise for Lin Jensen's
Bad Dog! A Memoir of Love, Beauty, and Redemption in Dark Places

"*Bad Dog!* is simply the best book on the wisdom of living I have seen in many years. Its honesty, insight, and pathos pull you into it the way good literature does. I strongly recommend this one."
—Thomas Moore, author of *Care of the Soul*

"Amazing."—*Turning Wheel*

"Lin Jensen writes with a deep understanding of life, the land, and the human spirit."—Christopher Moore, bestselling author of *Fluke*

"The tact and restraint in Jensen's writing match the keenness of observation and the rare beauty of expression, allowing the words to go deep."—Joanna Macy, author of *World as Lover, World as Self*

"An exquisite work of alarming lucidity."
—Stephen Batchelor, author of *Buddhism Without Beliefs*

"Lin Jensen demonstrates that seeing the world as it actually is means being fully alive."
—Sylvia Boorstein, author of *That's Funny, You Don't Look Buddhist*

"In *Bad Dog!*—which I wish everyone would read—Lin Jensen shows that kindness, forgiveness, and acceptance are necessary practices for anyone who wishes to be happy. They don't make life easy—but they make life possible."—*Chattanooga Pulse*

"Compellingly beautiful and inspiring."
—Keith Kachtick, author of *Hungry Ghost*

"Beautifully and powerfully written.
A hauntingly honest reminder to open our hearts."
—Ellen Birx, co-author of *Waking Up Together*

"A can't-put-it-down exploration of family love and pain."
—Susan Moon, author of *The Life and Letters of Tofu Roshi*

Praise for Lin Jensen's
*Pavement: Reflections on Mercy, Activism,
and Doing "Nothing" for Peace*

"This is a great book."
—Noah Levine, author of *Dharma Punx*

"With insight and refreshing simplicity Lin Jensen undermines
the illusion of futility that surrounds nonviolent activism. "
—Ethan Nichtern, director of The Interdependence Project (theidpro-
ject.com), and author of *One City*

"This is a truly inspirational book."
—*Spirituality & Practice*

"This book has been an almost-daily source of inspiration."
—WildMind Buddhist Meditation blog

"Jensen's gets to the pith of moments, to their deepest
implications, weaving in Zen parables and past experience as
necessary, all in the space of a few pages."
—*Tricycle*

"Riveting, gentle, tough, [and] funny. It's a gift to all suffering beings."
—*Chattanooga Pulse*

"Jensen is a skilled memoirist who articulates well the internal doubts
and fears that readers will reluctantly admit are familiar."
—*Shambhala Sun*

"The author of one of my very favorite books has done it again.
—Nancy Patton, editor of *Mandala*

Lin Jensen

Together Under One Roof
Making A Home of the Buddha's Household

WISDOM PUBLICATIONS • BOSTON

Wisdom Publications, Inc.
199 Elm Street
Somerville MA 02144 USA
www.wisdompubs.org

Library of Congress Cataloging-in-Publication Data
Jensen, Lin.
   Together under one roof : making a home of Buddha's household / Lin Jensen.
       p. cm.
   ISBN 0-86171-554-3 (pbk. : alk. paper)
   1. Religious life—Buddhism. 2. Jensen, Lin. I. Title. II. Title: Together under 1 roof.
   BQ5405.J47 2008
   294.3'444—DC22

                              2008016708

ISBN 0-86171-554-3
12 11 10 09 08
5 4 3 2 1

Cover design by Philip Pascuzzo. Interior design by Dede Cummings. Set in bulmer MT 12/15.

Earlier forms of seven chapters herein have appeared in the following periodicals: "Keeping an Ear to the Ground," "Washing Bowls," "Public Ethics," "Fair and Foul" in *Tricycle*; "How Civilization Is Made" in *Turning Wheel*; "Ten Thousand Mistakes" in *Shambhlala Sun*; "Molting" in *Mandala*.

Wisdom Publications' books are printed on acid-free paper and meet the guidelines for permanence and durability of the Production Guidelines for Book Longevity of the Council on Library Resources.

Printed in the United States of America.

This book was produced with environmental mindfulness. We have elected to print this title on 30% PCW recycled paper. As a result, we have saved the following resources: 15 trees, 11 million BTUs of energy, 1,327 lbs. of greenhouse gases, 5,507 gallons of water, and 707 lbs. of solid waste. For more information, please visit our website, www.wisdompubs.org. This paper is also FSC certified. For more information, please visit www.fscus.org.

To Karen Laslo,
whose good heart and intelligence
guide me through my days.

Contents

Acknowledgments

I THANK THE MANY TEACHERS who have preserved and taught the Dharma, for without their teaching I cannot imagine how I would have ever found my way beyond the confusion of wayward thought and feeling. Among those teachers whose lives have directly touched my own, I'm indebted to Soto Priest Katherine Thanas who on a summer evening in Carmel, California, first taught me to sit zazen. I'm also indebted to Reverend Master Jiyyu Kinnett and the community of Shasta Abbey monks whose manner of living together in true brotherhood and sisterhood taught me the genuine meaning of the Sangha Refuge. In addition I want to acknowledge my indebtedness to the teaching of John Tarrant, who introduced me to the Rinzai tradition and the pleasure and freedom of koan work. Finally, I'm indebted to Joanna Macy whose joyful and kindly presence lays healing hands upon the wounds we humans bear. Of those contemporary masters whose teaching has reached me solely through the medium of books, I'm especially indebted to Kosho Uchiyama, Zenkei Shibayama, and Shunryu

Suzuki. And as always, I give special thanks to Josh Bartok, Senior Editor of Wisdom Publications, whose wise guidance reaches beyond his invaluable editing, drawing out of me more than I thought myself capable of.

Where the Buddha Lives:
An Introduction

THE BUDDHA'S HOUSEHOLD encompasses the whole universe yet manifests in its entirety in single neighborhoods and individual houses. The Buddha's household is none other than our own and the Buddha has taken up residence there—and in our collective body and mind as well. We are one family under one roof sharing one mind.

Consider this fragment of ancient koan, one of the many teaching stories that characterize the long family history of Zen:

Chao-chou asked, "What is the Tao?"
Nan-ch'uan said, "Ordinary mind is the Tao."

The human mind is the universe's consciousness, the instrument through which the universe discerns its own presence and knows itself. And through Chao-chou's question, the universe is questioning itself, inquiring into the circumstances of its own nature. It's as if with the advent of the human mind, the universe had at long last shrugged off its primeval sleep and awakened, asking at long last "What am I?" Nan-ch'uan answers, for the whole universe, saying essentially, "*Just this* is what I am." Both question and answer are a consequence of the human capacity to reflect. We awakened here on this spinning planet in this inconceivable circumstance, only to discover that we *are* this very planet and circumstance. And from that awakening arose the deep and abiding human longing to know where we come from and where we belong. And it is this that spurred Chao-chou to ask of his teacher Nan-ch'uan, "What is the Tao?"—what is the way home? In our isolating self-awareness, we are like uprooted trees bearing with us a teasing recollection of native soil.

This longing for home is the basis of religious inquiry. Yet, ironically, it is a longing that often mistakenly takes us not nearer but farther from home, setting us out on mental pilgrimages of fanciful metaphor and grand aspirations. We abandon our place at the kitchen counter in favor of kneeling at temple altars. We leave off cooking and lawn mowing for the sake of ceremonial ritual. We light incense and don robes of black, of brown, of purple with gold brocade. We aspire to heaven in preference to earth. In short, we shun the ordinary.

While priests and teachers of many religious traditions offer the spiritual aspirant access to various exotic heavens, Zen offers a one-way ticket to the heaven of the ordinary. And while most religions aspire to a specialized state of mind, a state more holy than accorded to ordinary mind, Zen insists that the ordinary mind is as holy as it gets. When the Emperor Wu of China asked Bodhidharma, "What is the holiest principle of Buddhism?" Bodhidharma replied, "Nothing holy in it," refusing to isolate holiness in principle of any sort and leaving the Emperor with nothing but the ground under his feet.

Zen has been insistent on this matter. When students have asked various Zen masters "What is Buddha?"—a question tantamount to asking "What is God?" or "What is the Tao?"—the answers have invariably pointed to the most mundane possible circumstances:

Yunmen said, "A dried shitstick."
Ma-tsu said, "This very mind."
And a mature Chao-chou lived to say, "The oak tree in the courtyard."

An old story tells of a Zen master who was harvesting flax when a monk asked him this question. The master held up a handful of flax, showing the questioner that a handful of flax, the dirt under one's feet, or even one's soiled gloves is the living body of the Buddha. My teachers taught me to give to all my surroundings the same care and respect I might give to the temple altar. Every object you or I touch is Buddha, and every house—including a homeless shelter or a prison complex or the downtown mall with its sprawling parking lot—is the exact place where the Buddha takes up residence. And we are all keepers of the Buddha's house. The proper labors of a Buddhist begin and end right here on our own familiar, native ground.

D. T. Suzuki in *An Introduction to Zen Buddhism* tells of a monk named Yecho who asked, "What is Buddha?" and was told, "You are Yecho." Suzuki also reports another curious response of a master who simply answered, "No nonsense here." I particularly like this last response because it exemplifies Zen's overriding attitude of *no-sense* at all, not even nonsense, an attitude that resists ascribing unwarranted meaning or sense to reality itself. If Zen could be said to have a motto—and it can't!—the motto would be "Add nothing extra."

Zen is pared down to a simple household thing—and its practice applies to the place where we actually live out our lives. Buddhism in general is a religion that asks us to stay at home where we can attend to our lives firsthand and are truly present in our own skins, honoring the mind and body we were born with. While the old monks followed a tradition of leaving home (so split up a lot of families), they ironically managed nonetheless to preserve the attributes of household in their several temples, monasteries, and encampments.

Followers of Buddhism have always been studious to engage the ordinary lives and labors of human life. Huineng, for example, who would eventually become the sixth Zen ancestor, was first put to work in the harvesting shed to husk rice before receiving the attention of his teacher. A monk newly arrived to Nan-ch'uan's monastery came upon the master working in the garden one day, and not knowing he was addressing the master himself, asked, "What is the way to Nan-ch'uan?" Nan-ch'uan held up his sickle and said, "This sickle costs thirty cents." The monk said, "I didn't ask about a sickle. I asked about the way to Nan-ch'uan." Nan-ch'uan added, "It cuts very well." Seeking instruction in the Buddha Way, the monk received exactly that. This very sickle, this grass, this simple labor is the truth you're looking for.

In our human capacity for self-reflection and personal assessment, we have felt the hunger of the spirit for its home and have tended to look toward the heights—toward Olympus, Sinai, Sumeru; toward celestial cities of gold; toward the promise of imagined utopias of rest and spiritual fulfillment. But we have done so at the neglect of the spirit's true home. We have disparaged the heaven of the ordinary in favor of wholly fanciful and insubstantial abstractions. But the living spirit is not so airy a thing. In order to live, spirit requires a body and a place of the concrete sort that makes up the everyday pattern and substance of our actual lives.

It is good that we are filled with wonder. It is good that we long for the site of our heart's true realm. It is from this longing that this book, *Together Under One Roof*, has taken shape. My wish is that its chapters will help to restore us, you and me, to our own natural selves, and that together we will all realize that wherever we are we're already at home and that our ordinary mind is, in fact, the Tao.

Naming Buddha

THE ZAFU I SIT ON for meditation is a round pleated cushion made of heavy black cloth and filled with buckwheat hulls. It's about a foot in diameter with a four-inch loft. While all Buddhists take refuge in the Buddha, it's taught that the true Buddha can't be named. But that's not so, because I've already said, "zafu"—but I could just as well say "license plate" or "Aunt Mildred" or "stocking cap" or "butterfly." The truth is I can't avoid saying the Buddha's name because that's all there is to say.

In his ninth *Duino Elegy*, Rainer Maria Rilke wonders if this sort of saying isn't the very thing humans were meant to do. "Perhaps," Rilke writes, "we are here in order to say: house, bridge, fountain, gate, pitcher, fruit tree, window—at most: column, tower . . . But to say them, you must understand, Oh to say them more intensely than the things themselves ever dreamed of existing." I might wish for something grander to say than "fruit tree" or "window," but if I say these things truly I will have taken residence in the very house where Buddha has set up housekeeping. Rilke, writing in a Christian religious tradition, warns that you can't impress an angel with transcendent ideas and feelings. Better, he says, to "show him something simple. Tell him of things. He will stand astonished." The astonishment occurs when the *ideal* of the matter comes up against the *fact* of the matter, when the absolute confronts the unique genius of the actual. And when that happens, there's nothing more astonishing than a thing.

The thought that we humans are here on earth in order to write a sort of vocabulary of reality touches me with a sense of wonder and creative obligation. How did this talent for attaching words to fact ever come to pass? Who actually does the naming and what guides the shape and disclosure of the subsequent lexicon? All I know is that words come to me, if at all, in the language of actual things, the vocabulary of which is a kind of verbal net cast on the waters of an otherwise incomprehensible current of chance occurrence. We fleshly, earth-bound creatures are writing a language of creation, word by word. It's really quite wonderful. Of course, the Buddha is right to caution against mistaking the word for a thing for the thing itself. And it's also true that the thing itself remains ineffable regardless of its having been named. But still words play themselves out in the orchestra of the mind like lyrics written for the "music of the spheres" that the medieval mystics once heard.

There must have been a time when the nameless being that materialized in the space above the crib, taking me up in its arms and offering its nourishing nipple to my thirst, was first known by me as *mother*, a time when *parent* and *child* fit themselves to my tongue and it became possible for me to reflect on the nature and meaning of such a relationship. With instruments of investigation, we have penetrated the substructure of reality to a diminishing point that only the language of mathematics speaks, and we have penetrated outward to the faintest blinking light in some far galaxy of the universe and named it *star*. Putting names to things, rather than taming the world by substituting language for living fact, infuses the world with a wild wonderment known only to creatures who trade in words.

I WAS AND STILL AM TO SOME EXTENT A BIRDER, having once served as a sub-regional editor for *American Birds* magazine, covering the bird populations of Plumas and Sierra counties in northeastern California. I've spent a lot of time in the field observing and listing the birds I see. Most birders keep a "life list" of bird species they've sighted in their lifetime, an activity that can become keenly competitive, with the more determined competitors racing about in search of one more bird species to add to their life list than anyone else has been able to add. But listing has another quality as well. Listing is one way to keep faith with reality, a reduction of an event to its barest certainties (a certain species on a certain day in a certain place). Bird listing in this way is an insistence on seeing and recording things exactly as they are. The lister names what he sees, and in doing so bestows upon the things of this world a quality of intimate observation that I personally equate with love.

Angels, as Rilke pointed out, know nothing of the intensity of human love. They are but an airy abstraction of the mind, a weak and distant generalization of the fact at hand. Show an angel a Brewer's Sparrow or Hermit Thrush or Stellar's Jay and he will stand astonished. Call it by name and you will have identified his entire universe in a flutter of feathers and hollowed bones darting among the leaves.

The mystery of our existence doesn't lie in what is hidden but in what is not—not in the unnamed but in the very capacity to name anything at all. Though Buddhism, particularly Zen, makes much of the transmission *beyond* words, little is ever said of the transmission *by* words. Among the Dharma books I treasure most—the *Gateless Barrier, Blue Cliff Record*, Zenkei Shibayama's *A Flower Does Not Talk*, Kosho Uchiyama's *Opening the Hand of Thought*—is included an unabridged dictionary of the English language. I open it at random and find myself among entries for the letter *D*. My eyes fall on *double-disc harrow*, and I learn that it is "a harrow with two sets of discs so arranged that one set throws soil outward and the other throws it inward." I read this and I taste anew the long day's labor in the fields of turned earth that account for every bite of my evening meal. A *doubler*, I'm told, is "a textile worker who doubles thread or folds cloth, usually by machine," an entry that teaches me a little more about how I got the shirt on my back. I throw the dictionary open to another section and discover the term *isostatic*, which is the state of being "subjected to equal pressure on every side," and I'm reminded of the most visible and ordinary miracle of equilibrium.

Buddha-nature is a mystery that declares itself in plain sight, and since it is a mystery that manifests solely in the things of this world, it can be named. My unabridged dictionary records the long and ongoing history of that naming. The lexicographer walks a path as sacred and profound as any path we humans have undertaken. And we all walk that path with him, because language is shaped unwittingly in the mouths of those who speak it.

Whatever else we humans are, we are first and foremost sages of the word.

Defending Earth

THERE ARISES FROM WITHIN the deeper meditations of Zen the realization that the surface of the skin is not a boundary between self and other. When that happens, the whole universe becomes an extension of self or, more accurately, the self becomes realized as an extension of the universe in an experience of integration so radical that Thich Nhat Hahn has coined the word *inter-being* to describe the condition. As a verb, it can be conjugated: I *inter-am*, she *inter-is*. We inter-are with all things—and this perception constitutes a radical environmentalism that argues a necessary defense of the earth. It is a defense that concurs with the Buddhist practice of nonharming. "All living things are one seamless body," an old scripture tells us. For the Zen Buddhist, this scripture is both a truth and an obligation. As a truth it's self-evident and can't easily be set aside. As an obligation, it guides our hand in all we do, for we realize that whatever we touch—sentient or non-sentient, scaled, feathered, furred, or fleshed—is one body, and that one body is our own.

Of course Buddhists have no monopoly on such feelings of connectedness. We humans are creatures of nature ourselves and have a deep and abiding affinity with the natural world. There must have been a time when we all recognized the earth and ourselves as extensions of one another, a time when our actions toward nature necessarily reflected the dependence and kinship we share with other creatures. Even now, this deeper realization must lie dormant somewhere beneath the tragic overlay of a century of human disregard of an abused, forgotten, and neglected earth. Buried beneath the successive and accumulating layers of sedimentary rock, it took ten hundred million years for the leaves that brushed the dinosaur's flanks to be pressed and heated into a lake of petroleum. Had we not chanced upon this vast reservoir of stored power things might have gone differently than they have. But with such unprecedented capabilities in hand, we unleashed the very force of nature *against* nature, measuring as gain an unspeakable and irreversible plundering of the land.

The proper defense of the earth is not found in protective custody but in relinquishment. What's needed most of all is the will to leave the earth alone and let it unfold in its own time and way. Ironically, wars—which are so often fought over who holds title to some disputed piece of land—are particularly destructive of land. In the aftermath of any modern war of sufficient scale, vast territories of countryside and city lie in ruins, poisoned by military ordinance of various sorts, and sometimes virtually uninhabitable for decades.

The actions of industry as well often comprise little less than a violent attack upon the earth. Factories belch poisonous carbon residues into the atmosphere until the surrounding skies darken and nearby mountains disappear. A yellowing sun glows dismally through the brown haze, and people cough and wheeze and look out through watering eyes. Frequent air pollution reports advise people, in regard for their health, to not go outdoors at all. The water of rivers that once ran clear and drinkable is rendered so poisonous by our human discharge that we would die of self-poisoning were we to drink it without first putting it through elaborate and costly water treatment procedures. The fish, with no such option, simply die off, leaving behind a river that is itself dead.

It's been our tragedy to forget where and by what means we live. Yet, there are those among us who haven't forgotten; there are those who, because the earth can't speak for itself, have chosen to speak for it. And because the earth is ultimately vulnerable to the relentless pressures brought to bear upon it, there are those who will jeopardize the safety of their own lives in its protection.

In Thailand, Buddhist monks came to the defense of the nation's rainforests that had been brought to the edge of extinction by the logging interests of Western corporations. It so happened that the logging companies depended on village workers to cut down the trees. And while the villagers needed the work, they were also devotional Buddhists. So what the monks did was to enter the forests slated for logging where they performed ceremonies of ordination for several representative trees, chanting and draping the trees in ceremonial robes. The villagers, seeing the trees honored as Dharma brothers and sisters, refused to cut them down. To do so was seen as striking one's own flesh.

Those who have dedicated themselves to the defense of the earth have followed, with rare exception, a tradition of resistance that is nonviolent. In defense of the great whales, they have put themselves in the path of the whaler's harpoon; in defense of the rainforest, they have chained themselves to trees; in defense of the old-growth redwoods of the Pacific Northwest, they have climbed into the high branches and refused to return to ground for as long as two year's duration; in defense of wetlands and vernal pools, they have lain down in the path of the bulldozers. Their means of defense is to make themselves as vulnerable as the things they strive to protect, knowing that the body of earth is indivisible from their own.

Ultimately the defense of the earth is a defense of one's self.

OF ALL THE MUNICIPAL WATERSHEDS in this nation of ours, perhaps the most degraded of them is that of the Los Angeles Basin. The fifty-two mile length of the Los Angeles River that once meandered through a lush riparian corridor, spawning vast wetlands on its approach to the sea, has been reduced to a concrete drainage ditch stripped of all its vegetation, crisscrossed by a series of jammed freeways crawling with cars, lined by industrial plants, warehouses, and railroad yards. Backed up to the elevated cement levees and sandwiched between junkyards, gravel plants, and oil refineries are some of the poorest immigrant neighborhoods in the entire basin, remnants of what was once the original Pueblo de Los Angeles. Like the river, these inhabitants have been essentially discarded, put out of mind in favor of more profitable interests. But it is from these forgotten neighborhoods on the banks of this forgotten river that one of the most heartening defenses of the natural world has arisen.

They call themselves the River School, and they consist of middle school and high school students formed into teams to monitor what's left of the river in hopes of encouraging its unlikely restoration. Under the hum of high-voltage power lines and the sizzle of tires on an adjacent freeway, a group of teenagers with notebooks stand and look down the concrete inner slope of the levee to the floor of the river where the cement once laid down by the Army Corps of Engineers has cracked and split open to allow a trickle of stagnant water to ooze up out of the mud. A smear of green algae has gathered there and a few scrubby willows have taken root.

These children, deprived of contact with much of anything natural, find this small oasis in a degraded riverbed a thing of beauty. When they find a few crayfish clinging to the algae, they're thrilled with the discovery.

A thirteen-year-old named Brenda says, "My friends don't believe I went to the L.A. River! They're like, there's nothing there, that's a sewer! I used to think it was a sewer, too, but when I went there, it was beautiful." Another time she said, "The best bird I saw was the blue heron, a beautiful bird—I loved the blue." And the thing is, Brenda's right. The heron *is* beautiful. The slightest resurrection of nature under such unlikely circumstances *is* beautiful. And Brenda's delighted "I loved the blue" is as beautiful as it ever gets. Recalling a day when she and some others were tugging a heavy load of trash up out of the river channel, Brenda said, "I started to think, 'Oh my God, I could be cleaning up my own trash!' Gum or a piece of paper or something you threw out. It gave me a whole different look on the world." And Daniel, a classmate of Brenda's said, "You can see plants coming through the cement— and that explains a lot. Nature is trying so very hard to be alive."

Nature *is* trying hard to be alive. And so are these offspring of the poverty-ridden, pavement-and-graffiti neighborhoods trying hard to be alive. They somehow know that their own survival is to be found in the resurrection and survival of the river.

The last frame of the Ten Ox-herding Pictures—a traditional series of teachings depicting the unfolding of the spiritual path— shows the newly enlightened bodhisattva re-entering the town of his birth with life-saving hands, offering the joy and wisdom of his own awakening to any who choose to follow. Surely these enlightened youngsters descending into the scummy muck of what was once the Los Angeles River, clutching in their life-saving hands an assortment of trash bags and notebooks, measuring sticks and sampling vials, are the bodhisattvas of our times. Their innocent delight in discovering there the least thing that still survives and grows is a measure of the heart's own native wisdom. Their seemingly hopeless undertaking to save the river measures the courage of the bodhisattva's vow to save all beings.

The River School volunteers beckon to us to follow. Their salvation, and ours, and that of the earth itself, depends on whether we will go with them or not.

The Iron Flute with No Holes

I ONCE HAD THE PRIVILEGE to train under the guidance of John Tarrant, a truly supple and imaginative koan master. In the years I spent with John he taught me how to let the koan draw me out of abstract thought and into the living moment, which is another way to say that he taught me how to let the koan set my mind free of logical constraints—to "play the iron flute with no holes," as an ancient koan urges.

A mind tossed up against the illogicality of such a proposition either shrinks away from it altogether or breaks into the sheer freedom it offers. If the mind shrinks away, it does so by retreating within the limits of the conceivable, where boundaries are clearly designated and spiritual progress is linear and defined in rational stages. If the mind breaks into the freedom of the koan, it takes hold of the impossibility of playing such a flute and plays it anyway. Because it can't be played at all, it can be played in any way one likes. With such an instrument everything is potential, nothing is yet formed or determined. The flute has no mouthpiece to put our lips to or holes to fit our fingers to. No song has yet been written for it. But when the music breaks upon the ear, our journey into the impossible will have brought us home to the surprising originality and genius of the ordinary mind.

My friend David refers to the place where genius and originality abide as "the empty field with no signposts." When I reminded David that Master Hung-chih had given us the empty field part of the image as far back as the tenth century, he'd never heard of Hung-chih. "Then where did you get it?" I asked. "I got it from the field," he said. Of course, I thought, the same place Hung-chih got it. We humans don't invent the empty field, we discover it.

In such a field there'd be no freeway off-ramps. In fact, the territory would have yet to be surveyed and no maps drawn for it. Finding yourself in the empty field, you could move in all 360 degrees of possible direction. One can easily see the connection between the images of the iron flute, the empty field, and the Buddhist term *emptiness*, inasmuch as all three are terms that connote a circumstance or reality without limiting characteristics. Emptiness comprises all things in their uniqueness and is therefore not confined to any one thing at all. Still, it's not that uncommon to find myself once again walking in perfect emptiness while on the hunt for it, mistaking it for something other than what's clearly at hand. When I do this, perhaps I imagine emptiness is something I can get hold of, a Zen collectible of a sort.

Yen-yang, a Chinese monk of old, apparently felt this way, and in his pride of accomplishment, he came to an interview with Zen Master Chao-chou saying, "I don't bring a single thing. How about that?" Chao-chou said, "Put it down." Yeng-yang said, "If I don't bring a single thing, what should I put down?" Chao-chou said, "In that case, carry it away." Indeed, Yen-yang's notion of emptiness was one of something he could have or not have, which seems logical enough until you find yourself encumbered with an "empti-ness" that can be neither put down nor carried away. In the same way, the iron flute can be neither played nor not played, and the impossibility of it persists until you realize that you *are* emptiness itself, you *are* the flute. That's when the great space opens up and the music breaks on your ear. The point that interests me most in all this is how much of what we humans think and choose and do, believing our thoughts, choices, and actions to be determined by rational consideration and therefore logical, aren't in fact logical and rational at all. Koan practice invites us to acknowledge the extent of what we don't know. A koan undermines certainties and invites doubt.

One of Master Pa-ling's three turning words was the koan "What is the blown-hair sword?" When I was given this koan, my teacher explained that the blown-hair sword has a blade so sharp it would cut a single hair blown against it. So what is the blown-hair sword? While as many different answers might be given to the question as there are people to give them, the sharpest sword I know of is the sword of doubt. It cuts away every fixed assurance my mind invents. It exposes the arbitrary nature of my most care-fully reasoned conclusions. It undermines my every attempt to get it right, leaving me without a single unassailable truth or belief to rely on. With everything cut away and nothing intact, what's left to me is too alive for belief or certainty of any sort. It's the moment where I take the unformed flute in hand and, without a clue as to how it might be done, genuinely consider playing a tune on it. The resultant melody is a freedom born of radical doubt and is as close as I can come to naming emptiness. Yet the term *emptiness* in its common usage rarely invokes the freshness and space that arrive when one steps into the actual void, which is always the birthplace of the next moment. It is the peculiar power of the koan to return us again and again to that field of birth where we walk in wonderment and continual surprise. You might not consider it particularly surprising or wonderful to be in the kitchen cutting up carrots and potatoes for the evening's vegetable stew. And that's okay. We can't expect to be dazzled by the improbability of everything we do. In fact, your being there getting supper together might seem perfectly logical and ordinary. But the thing about "logical and ordinary" is that nothing ever really is logical and ordinary. You could probably produce a rationale as to why you happen to be in this kitchen at this particular time and age with this particular knife in hand, but if you allow the slightest doubt to arise regarding this otherwise perfectly reasonable account, you'll be quickly brought to realize that you have no idea why you happen to be where you are. You might be surprised to find yourself there at all. You will have cut away plausibility itself, and in that sweet vacancy, given birth to the impossible right there in your own kitchen.

"Now You Stop Too."

*I*N THE STATE OF CALIFORNIA, where I live, thirteen death row inmates have been executed since 1976 and 652 more are awaiting execution. In Texas, 379 inmates have been put to death in the same period and 404 wait their turn. The suicide rate among U.S. death row inmates is 113 per every 100,000 sentenced to die, ten times the rate of suicide among the general population. High Desert State Prison, where I serve as Senior Buddhist Chaplain, houses 4,000 inmates—twice the capacity for which the prison was built. And 2,400 of them are serving life sentences. Most of them are young, eighteen to twenty-five years old, and they won't even be considered for possible parole until they're in their mid-forties to mid-fifties. Most of them will never leave prison. Unless you go to see them and look into their faces, as I do, these castoffs of our society are out of sight and out of mind. They're the ones we've given up on. As one sergeant on the prison guard staff put it to me, "What we've got here is the scum of the earth." While there may be reasonable causes for locking someone up for life or putting someone to death, the truth is that we as a society do these things to be rid of people we don't want to deal with and don't want around. They're felons, we tell ourselves, and deserve to be shunned by decent people. We find it easiest to just discard what offends us.

This kind of exclusion operates on a collective as well as individual level, often shaping national policies and influencing the attitudes of the populations of entire countries. In the mid-1980s Ronald Reagan and a following of U.S. conservatives dubbed the Soviet Union the "Evil Empire." Americans readily took up the phrase. An entire region with all its divergent customs, histories, and geographical differences was shunned and set aside as "evil," just like the evil Galactic Empire in Star Wars which had served as the inspiration for Reagan's choice of terms. George W. Bush, displaying the same tragically impoverished imagination as that of Reagan, declared in his January 2002 State of the Union Address that the nations of Iran, Iraq, and North Korea constituted an "axis of evil." And on May sixth of the same year, Undersecretary of State John R. Bolton extended the condemnation to include Lybia, Syria, and Cuba, which he termed nations "beyond the axis of evil."

The poverty of Reagan, Bush, and Bolton's imaginations lies in their narrowness, their capacity to enfold the populations of six nations into one slim conceptualization. "States like these, and their terrorist allies," Bush told the nation, "constitute an axis of evil, aiming to threaten the peace of the world." You can see that it's not that these government leaders have *no* imagination, they have in fact invented for themselves a fiction so grand, and one of which they are so certain, that the whole world is reeling from its repercussions. The purpose served by contriving plots of such standardized simplification is to rid oneself of having to deal with the realities of other people's lives and behaviors. It's a method of getting rid of people by isolating them within a convenient stereotype. It allows you to simply discard them, to cast them out.

The ancient and repeated tale of casting out wrongdoers, of shunning and discarding other's lives, unfolds in a plot of suffering and hatred. It is a tale that hardens the mind and prevents one from understanding the circumstances of others, a tale of arrogance and pride and disregard. When I judge harshly of others and set them aside as though unworthy of further consideration, I need to look at my own wrongs and ask who it is I want to exclude. When I remember to do this, a kindness visits me that allows me to acknowledge that the mistakes of others are my own mistakes as well.

In the Zen tradition in which I train, as in all Buddhist traditions, there is no such person as an outcast. Everyone is included. The Buddha acted on this sense of merciful inclusion when he took the serial killer, Angulimala, into the Sangha as a Dharma brother. The story goes that Angulimala had been stalking the Buddha for hours, intending that monk to be his next and final victim, the last of a series of murders he'd set out to commit. When he overtook the Buddha, he came upon him from behind only to find him sitting in deep meditation. He didn't want to kill a man engaged in what he took to be a religious practice—and so Angulimala waited. Time passed and still the monk persisted in his meditation. Finally no longer able to constrain himself, Angulimala cried out in frustration, "Stop, monk, stop!" The exact moment of acknowledgment and inclusion is captured when the silent meditating monk turned slowly, and "like a compassionate father to his prodigal son, said 'I have stopped, Angulimala, now you stop too.'"

The Buddha's simple words and powerful presence called to Angulimala's better self and his murderous aim was averted on the instant and he was suddenly deeply repentant. He spent the rest of his life as a Sangha-member trying to mend in others the violence he had known in himself. Yet he was never freed of the consequences of his earlier murderous acts. We are told "he was distrusted by the villagers, who frequently refused to help him during his alms rounds, pelting him instead with stones." Having once seen himself in the eyes of the Buddha, he stood his ground, accepting his punishment, witnessing to his tormentors that he was Angulimala, the murderer, and saying in effect, "I have stopped. Now you stop too."

It doesn't take any great wisdom to know that until you stop doing something, you're still doing it. As long as you keep on lying, you're a liar. Until you stop killing, you're a killer. And there's no guarantee that just because *you've* stopped, others will stop too. Inclusion makes one vulnerable. This is the cost that mercy exacts of the merciful. Angulimala might very well have killed the Buddha. No doubt the Buddha understood that and yet chose to leave his guard down and accept death if that's what was to come of it. And what was it, if not this tender and yielding courage of the Buddha, that so touched Angulimala that he was forever transformed by it? Kill me if you must, Angulimala, but I will not discount you as my brother. The story of Angulimala is a fanciful tale that speaks literal truth.

At High Desert State Prison, I meet many Angulimalas. Some among them have come upon the Buddha and he has told them to stop. Surely each of us who follow the Buddha Way know of those moments in our lives when the Buddha appeared and told us to stop. Such a moment is an encounter with our own greater heart, a heart that denies none and takes all within its keeping, a heart that doesn't give up on anyone regardless of what he or she might have done. It is this loving mercy that we forfeit when we shun others or discard them for their wrongs, putting them out of sight and mind.

As I write this, my nation, the United States of America, continues to market for popular consumption words and phrases designed to allow for the easy identification of outcasts. In addition to the highly popular "axis of evil," which won an eighty percent approval rating for the invasion of Iraq, are now added such new coinages as "Islamic extremist," and "insurgent," terms which apply to any Muslim determined to fight back, and of course the ever expanding and flexible term of "terrorist," which has come to include just about anyone who disagrees with administrative foreign policy. And here at home, we still believe that anyone who has done serious wrong is a "felon" and therefore should be locked up or put to death. Categorical words like these support a simple dichotomy of good and evil, and encourage people to think in terms of a stark opposition between *us* and *them.*

I take it as an obligation to resist such exclusionary terms, seeking instead a language that is inclusive and doesn't relegate others to a status of indifference and disregard. I further take the merciful and forgiving heart of the Buddha as a model of behavior. Surely if the Buddha could open his heart to the very one who'd come seeking his death, I should be able to find some degree of understanding and compassion for those who might threaten me with harm. It's an unfortunate habit of the human mind to take sides, dividing up society on the basis of arbitrary standards. It's a persistent habit that insinuates itself into language and spreads its influence by that means to others. To the degree that it's a habit of my own behavior, I'm determined to stop. Perhaps, if I succeed, others will be encouraged to stop too.

Holding Place

A SHAMBHALA TEACHER ONCE TOLD ME to "hold my place." I'd gone to him for help in a matter in which I felt confusion and uncertainty. It was years ago, when I'd first been put to the task of founding and teaching a local Zen sangha, and I was feeling apprehensive with the responsibility of it. I told the Shambhala teacher of this, and he simply said, "Hold your place." "Yes," I said, "but . . ." And the teacher cut me off in mid-sentence, saying once again, "Hold your place." I realized then that he wasn't telling me what I might do at some future time when I was back home teaching the sangha. He meant hold your place *right now.* We both of us sat cross-legged, facing each other, and for a long time neither of us moved. It was then that I actually saw the teacher peering over the top of his bifocals and the walls of the room seemed suddenly present and I felt the solid floor beneath me. In that moment the distressing portent of future embarrassment and failure dissolved and I took my proper place in life once again. It wasn't that I was suddenly assured of being the Zen teacher I might wish to be, it was just that I understood then that I could accommodate whatever circumstances I found myself in by simply remembering to *hold my place*.

Holding place is not so much a stubborn refusal to budge (though on occasion it might be) as it is a willingness to set up housekeeping in the quarters you've been given. Household, I've discovered, is never any place other than where I happen to be. I either make my home there or not at all. I didn't ask to be born into a poor immigrant household, but finding myself there I had no other household in which to shape the mind and behavior that would carry me into the rest of my life. I didn't ask to fall in love, but when my love alighted on the person of Karen Laslo, there was nowhere else for my heart to take up residence. I didn't ask to be a Zen teacher either, but once put to it, the only alternative to failing the task was to hold my place. I suppose I'm laboring an obvious tautology in pointing out that by whatever combination of choice or chance we happen to arrive where we are, *that's where we are.* We have no other place to hold.

When holding place is an action taken in support of protest or advocacy, it frequently takes the form of a refusal to go away or be put out of sight somewhere. Workers, striking for union rights in early industrial America, would take to the streets to protest the conditions of employment. And when the company militias would charge the lines of workers with clubs and fixed bayonets, leaving many dead and many more staggered and wounded from the blows and stabbings they'd endured, the remnant of workers, patched up with bandages and refusing to go away, would be back on the street within a matter of hours. The women championing women's suffrage took their cause to the very gates of the nation's White House. They too were beaten and hauled off to prison, their banners and posters ripped up or burned, but they were back with fresh replacements almost as soon as the jeering crowd had dispersed. They would not be ignored or put out of sight, and stood their ground at the White House gates where the whole world could see them, holding their place until the president and the nation were shamed into capitulating to their rightful demand for the vote. When Martin Luther King was jailed in Birmingham in an effort to silence him, he managed to have scraps of paper smuggled to him and from the isolation of his cell wrote one of the world's classic declarations of equal rights, the "Letter From Birmingham Jail." Even under lock and key, he could not be put out of sight. At the very moment when Gandhi's call for Indian independence seemed doubtful of success and the British could speculate that they'd finally rid themselves of his aggravating presence, Gandhi, urging the refusal of British products, led his countrymen on a long march to the sea to make their own salt. The action led to such cruel abuses by British soldiers that the colonial powers were subsequently shamed into negotiating Indian independence.

While holding place is an act of body, it's a frame of mind as well. More precisely it's a mind without a frame. Every moment calls one into being anew. Holding place is the willingness to be born into that moment. Another way to put this is to say that the one who holds her place holds her question open. What would be best to do at this moment? She continually adjusts, not allowing her mind to settle on a fixed answer, knowing that it would draw her from her rightful place. In that sense, holding place is a continuing accommodation to present circumstance. Holding place is a practice of mindfulness, an awakening to the moment—but I want to acknowledge as well the concurrent sense of being bodily present in your life, trusting the body to hold its native ground.

Our bodies know where we belong even when we don't. If you feel out of place somewhere, rather than trying to figure out why, try following your feet. They may know the exact steps that will bring you back home to yourself. There's a deep pool in Chico Creek where the water flows over submerged granite boulders. It lays along my morning route where I go walking in the early dawn. It calls me into the waters on all but the coldest months of winter. I don't know why; and I don't ask. I trust my body to turn me aside from my walk and strip me of my shoes and clothing and plunge me into the chill water. And once there it's the only place for me to be. Hours afterward, I still feel the current flowing under and around me, brushing past my temples and filling my eyes. I bear through my days the vocabulary of water, a language that holds me in place.

Keeping an Ear to the Ground

WHEN ZEN MASTER IKKYU was asked, "What is Zen?" He replied, "Attention." When asked to elaborate, he said, "Attention! Attention! Attention!"

Ikkyu's words are an instruction in mindfulness, and mindfulness is commonly thought of by students as something you do on purpose. But Ikkyu's "attention" isn't necessarily what your fourth-grade math teacher had in mind when she caught you drifting off from the work at hand and told you to keep your mind on what you're doing. Such purposeful concentration might very well be the best advice in matters of an intellectual nature, but the mindfulness I have in mind is relaxed and freer than that, more a matter of simple wakefulness than anything else. It doesn't work very well to make a *project* out of mindfulness, because attention restricts itself and becomes selective when it's forced onto an object.

When I was first being instructed in the practice of zazen, I asked what I should do with my eyes since I was expected to meditate with my eyes at least partially open. "Look with a soft focus." I was told. "Don't stare at anything." And when I tried this, I found that, while I couldn't generate a soft focus by simply willing myself to do so, a soft focus would naturally arise all on its own so long as I didn't direct my attention toward anything in particular. In this way attention itself softens and I become more receptive to perceptions on the periphery of awareness. They slip in on me like an unintended smile that might appear on my face without my having necessarily noticed its presence there.

RECENTLY, ON A NOVEMBER MORNING, as I was outdoors raking up the fall leaves, a gardener hired by my neighbor was across the street raking leaves as well. He looked over at me, held up his rake, and waved. I held up my own rake and waved back. We both had grins on our faces. We were strangers to each other, having never met nor seen one another before. But we were two old men raking leaves, and he was moved by our common act to acknowledge the brotherhood we shared. I wasn't practicing mindfulness at the moment. I wasn't practicing anything at all. I was raking leaves. And I wasn't making a Buddhist project out of "staying in the now" either, though I've been instructed by teachers to do so. Yet a certain willing receptivity brought my raking companion and me to look up from our chores and join each other in a moment of affectionate regard.

This receptive quality of attention seems to me, or more accurately *feels* to me, akin to love, for we can only love what we allow ourselves to see. And it's not just other humans that elicit affection from us. I can testify to this in the most mundane way, as can any of us. But here's an example: I was once traveling in a car with a friend, and a mosquito kept buzzing around my face and neck until eventually I felt the telltale itch that told me the mosquito had fed. And then it appeared on the windshield of the car, its tiny body made translucent against the opposing sunlight. I could actually see a lit-tle red thread of my own blood shimmering inside the mosquito. I was touched with admiration and affection for this beautiful crea-ture whose eggs would feed on an offering of my own body. I said to my companion in the car, "Look, Frank, you can see my blood in the mosquito's body"—and before I could object, he'd smashed the mosquito with the flat of his hand, leaving nothing but a red smear on the glass. I don't blame Frank. I'd looked; he hadn't.

THE CRUX OF ZEN ETHICS equates simple mindfulness with the capacity to love, wherein a message is received from our own hearts and a natural affection arises from simply noticing things as they are. It is in the noticing that a connection is formed that lies deeper than language and thought and intention. In Sarah Orne Jewett's *The Country of the Pointed Firs* is a passage that aptly describes the nature of this living connection. Almiry Todd, a woman who could just as well be describing herself, says,

> There's sometimes a good hearty tree growin' right out of the bare rock, out o' some crack that just holds the roots, right on the pitch o' one of them bare stony hills where you can't seem to see a wheel-barrowfull o' good earth in a place, but that tree'll keep a green top in the driest summer. You lay your ear down to the ground an' you'll hear a little stream runnin'. Every such tree has got its own living spring; there's folk made to match 'em.

Ikkyu's attention is the living spring that nourishes the tree of awareness. It seeps in unawares and guides the human heart in all we do. While a Buddhist may cherish her vows to take up the way of the precepts and take guidance from what she's been taught, she nonetheless learns to keep her ear to the ground, listening to her own living spring and trusting that above all else. She receives the waters unwittingly like the cambium layer of cells in the stems and roots of some vascular plants, the living spring flowing into her from all sides—the scrape of shoes on the city street, the acceleration of cars, the studied precision of the cook cleaning the kitchen counter, the girl swinging her hair with a twist of her neck, the guard with his feet planted, an old woman's cough heard from an adjacent room, a hand nervously clenching and opening, the look in an eye, the tone a voice takes, a hesitation in mid-sentence, a child snatching at a pebble sunk in the creek. Her whole being is shaped to an instrument of loving attention. She doesn't accumulate these bits and facts of life like evidence on which to base a judgment. She doesn't accumulate anything at all, nor does she form an impression of what she sees and hears. She lets the world enter her body like sap rising from roots, trusting that the limbs will grow in their own way and the leaves unfold in time.

Elder Ting Stands Motionless

IN AN OLD ZEN STORY, Elder Ting asked Zen Master Lin-chi, "What is the great meaning of the Buddhist teaching?" Ting's question is one that seeks a durable truth, a greater security, in fact, than life is likely to afford anyone. In this life of uncertainty and unpredictability, Ting was asking for at least one unchanging truth, one stable proposition that could be held on to and relied upon. Lin-chi, in full respect of Ting's request, came down off his meditation seat and held Ting tightly and gave him a slap and pushed him away. Whatever response to his question Elder Ting had anticipated, it was surely not the one he got. And so with his old face still stinging from a slap across it, he stood motionless, not knowing what to do. It was then that a monk standing by said, "Elder Ting, why do you not bow?" Ting bowed. And in that moment, he understood that Lin-chi had answered his question. Startled from his initial quest, Elder Ting was offered the living moment instead. "Just this, Elder Ting, is the meaning you seek." What other meaning could there possibly be?

The moment when Elder Ting stood motionless is a moment of great promise and beauty. Whatever intention Ting brought to his interview with Lin-chi had been cancelled by the unexpected. His mind was swept free of purpose and he had nothing familiar at hand to tell him what to do. He was poised at the boundary of the unknown with no way of predicting where the next step would lead. As with Elder Ting, not knowing what to do is a circumstance that can jar any of us into wakefulness. This happens all the time, but we probably fail to notice it.

I don't necessarily have to be slapped in the face in order to wake up; I need only to be momentarily plucked up out of whatever comforting narrative I've designed for myself and dropped back into the world as it is. Encountering a grinning child with freckles and a missing baby tooth will easily do the trick, or a woman running in the park with her pigtails flopping from side to side, or a loosened leaf drifting down from overhead, or a man in a parking lot talking heatedly into a cell phone, or the call of Sandhill cranes passing overhead in the dark of night. When the world awakens me like this, all sorts of options appear that I had no idea were present before.

Like Elder Ting, I've had to learn to persevere in the face of the unexpected, resisting the urge to patch things back together, bowing to whatever circumstance has come upon me. If I can just hold still for a minute in the face of life's sometimes discomfiting surprises and not be quick to restore familiarity, that minute's pause will give birth to the next and my life will already have swung in directions I couldn't have foreseen. To allow life to unfold itself in its own way is to stay awake in the living moment, to resist is to rock myself to sleep with just another bedtime story. Sometimes the stories I tell myself are more comforting than the actual realities I'm faced with, but yielding to a convenient fiction forfeits the only life I can actually live.

A FRIEND OF MINE once surprised me with a disclosure I would never have suspected, and in doing so swept away my whole impression of an event we'd shared. I was invited along on an early summer hike with four friends into the high peaks of California's Sierra Nevada Range. I was new at hiking and a little apprehensive, but excited about the prospect. When I got to the trailhead and started up into the mountains, I found that my farm shoes weren't the best for the fields of snow we sometimes encountered and, while the other four had ice axes to secure them on steep slopes, I didn't. Once when I had to go on rope to lower myself down a cliff, I was initially frightened but, being reassured, did it without incident. The truth is I had a wonderful time, and came back feeling a deep comradeship with the others. We'd spent seven days in the mountains, and afterward I kept recounting in my mind the adventures we'd shared and the marvelous sights we'd seen.

A week later, when the four of us got together over supper to celebrate the trip, one of my hiking companions told me in the presence of the others that they'd thought I was a "real pain in the ass" at first but that I turned out okay after all. None of the other three countered this characterization. It felt to me like Lin-chi coming off the meditation seat to slap me in the face, and I was bewildered by it because I couldn't remember being a pain in the ass and didn't know whether I had been or not. I just thought we'd all had a good time together. And if not, then I didn't know what to do now with all the sweet memories of the trip I'd been treasuring and the affection I'd been feeling for my traveling companions.

I didn't argue the point or say anything in my defense. I just held still, which is a good thing probably but not something I can take credit for, because, you see, circumstances were such that I didn't know what else to do. I wasn't even sure at the moment whether my recollection of the trip was actually the way I remembered it or the way the others remembered it. Maybe I *had* been a pain in the ass. I just didn't know anymore. Because I had an entirely different version of the trip, the unfamiliar story they were telling was baffling to me. I felt thrust out of character into a role I didn't recognize and had no idea how to assume.

The point is that when circumstances snatched my prior realities away from me, it was useless to try and get them back or substitute some contrivance in their stead. All I could do was bow to the situation. And when I did, I freed myself from my part in the drama, watching it unfold as if it had nothing to do with me. It was then that I asked who this watcher of the drama was if not me. And I knew then that it didn't matter much whether my version of the trip or that of the others was the truth. I knew that I could always step aside from my own inventions, however comforting or painful they might be, and find a refuge in the one who oversees all inventions.

SOMETIMES SUCH SURPRISING SHIFTS are so seemingly inconsequential as to hardly warrant notice. I've had a lifetime aversion to eating oranges, for instance, which always perplexed and annoyed me, since they're such a good and available fruit. It wasn't that I was allergic to oranges and broke out in hives or anything; it's just that I couldn't stand the taste of them. I tried many times over the years to eat an orange, hoping each time that the taste wouldn't repulse me and I could add them to my diet. And then just this past year, at age 74, I picked up an orange, peeled it, broke off a section, and stuck it into my mouth. It tasted good! How does a thing like this happen? I've been eating oranges ever since, and while I can't say that I've become a fundamentally different person, I also can't say that I'm the same person who wasn't eating oranges.

Sometimes life will shift in unexpected ways that are pure celebration for the person involved. A Zen student of mine discovered rather suddenly a few years ago that he was truly and genuinely gay. He'd been talking to me for some time about whether he was bisexual or heterosexual. Sometimes he thought he might be feeling a sexual attraction to women. But when he followed up on this, he and the woman always became friends and a sexual relationship never developed. But he wasn't sure that he was gay either, and so he often spoke to me of his confusion. "I'm lonely," he said, "and I don't know what to do about it." Then he decided to accept an invitation to a gay retreat that a confidant of his had told him about— and so he drove over to Santa Rosa to see what would come of it. I saw him the day he got back. "I'm queer as a three-dollar bill!" he exclaimed, beaming with pleasure over the disclosure.

Buddhism, especially Zen, makes a big deal out of present circumstances being "just this," just what they are and not something else. This was the lesson that Lin-chi offered Elder Ting when he came seeking the great meaning of Buddhist teaching. But "just this" is an ever-shifting landscape, and so no meaning, great or otherwise, will long apply to any particular circumstance. I have to be willing to let go of the meanings I attribute to things, however cherished these meanings might seem. I've learned to value the surprises life brings me, even when they pull me loose from familiar moorings and set me adrift. I'd rather float free on an improbable sea of unfamiliar possibilities than seek security in a safe harbor of my own ideas. Besides, I'm less interested now in my ideas about things and more interested in the things themselves—and the things themselves are never what I think they are. They're always only themselves, unexpected and never the same.

Next!

I ONCE CHALLENGED David O'Keefe, the Chico Zen Sangha's practice leader, to bring forth the mind that dwells nowhere. David simply said, "Next!" I've never gotten a response I liked better.

Students given this koan will variously give a shout, "*Hya!*" or raise Chu-chih's one finger, or resort to "Mu" or indicate the clapping of one hand, or dance about or yawn or scratch to indicate an unrehearsed and spontaneous action of a sort. David's "Next!" didn't pause to bother with any of this. David's "Next!" had already turned the corner without marking the spot left behind.

In Shunryu Suzuki's classic work, *Zen Mind, Beginner's Mind*, he refers to beginner's mind as our "original mind" which he goes on to say, "is always rich and sufficient within itself." It is, he says, "actually an empty mind and a ready mind." It makes sense that an empty mind would be a ready mind, rich and sufficient, because, dwelling nowhere, an empty mind has nothing outside itself to lean on and because its very emptiness is an unrealized potential where possibility exists. An innocent and radical receptivity characterizes the mind of Zen, which never becomes accomplished or skilled at doing its work.

ALTHOUGH WORRY is typically an anxious effort to prepare for some future event, a worried mind is not a ready mind—it's too busy planning ahead. If I'm planning for what comes next, whatever comes has already slipped by without my noticing it. I often fret in this way over the repeated wars and trenchant violence that mark our species, turning us against one another. For example, I might try to figure out in advance what response would be best should a heated argument break out in a crowd somewhere, with name-calling and other verbal abuses that threatened to turn violent if not stopped. If the violence were imminent, would it be best for me to simply shout "Stop!" or call 911 or risk physical intervention, or would it be better to speak calmly in an effort to rein in the anger and bring circumstances under more reasonable control? I find myself rehearsing all sorts of potential scenarios like these to have ready should an opportunity ever arise to do anything at all. No matter how serious and justified these worried schemes of mine might be, they're unlikely to help much when I'm called upon to act. Even the best strategies and plans, as fit for an anticipated occasion as they might seem, can get in the way when discrete momentary choice and action are required.

This exact moment is forever the time for a beginner's mind, the mind that dwells nowhere. When the call comes to act I'm better off without all the good and wise ideas I've stored up in advance, thinking to have them ready when needed. What's actually needed is simple attention, a readiness without preconception. There's no prepared text that will suffice. David has something to say about this as well and recommends "starting from scratch," which is a

barnyard term for me that puts me in mind of fields freshly fur-
rowed in preparation for planting or of chickens pecking at the
scratch grain I've thrown them. They cluck about in the dirt, snap-
ping up bits of corn, millet, oats, and barley with a particular
chicken-like precision. And yet the chickens are perfect amateurs—
after all, a newly hatched chick when it is nothing but a tiny ball of
fuzz on twiggy legs will peck as well as the oldest hen in the flock.

Life doesn't ask of me that I come to it better prepared or
accomplished than a newly hatched chick. It only asks that I enter
each new moment at the very beginning of my life. When the shell
cracks open as it does all the time, all I need to do is step out into
the yard.

Or, as David puts it, "Next!"

Making Good Time

*Y*OGI BERRA, commenting on the human circumstance, said, "We appear to be lost. But we're making good time!" I think Yogi got it right. Making good time may be the best we can hope for, because we don't really seem to know where we're going.

Pema Chödrön tells of the time she first met her teacher, Chögyam Trungpa. He told everyone present that, if they'd come to get their act together, they should just forget it because they never would. Why do I find Trungpa's statement so hopeful when it would appear to damn the least hope one might possibly retain? It may seem strange to you that I would put it this way, but Trungpa's statement seems to me exactly the kind of encouragement the world needs more of. "Getting your act together" has about it a once-and-for-all sort of solidity and doesn't account for the conflicting exigencies we must negotiate in ordinary life. I think those who heard Trungpa that day must have come away reassured by these words of his, knowing that they weren't expected to be someone other than they were and that it was possible to live in the world as it is.

Trungpa's words echo those of the Buddha's First Noble Truth. Suffering exists, the Buddha said. We are all of us, he pointed out, subject to sickness, old age, and death. We will all suffer our share of pain, sorrow, and loss. None of us will escape having some of our best hopes cancelled by failure and disappointment. It was a relief for me to hear it put this way because if suffering is universal and unavoidable, then my own suffering isn't something gone wrong, something that shouldn't happen and needs to be fixed. The Buddha saw that as long as we humans resisted the chance misfortunes certain to overtake us, as long as we found the fact of suffering too grave a consequence to admit, our whole lives would be one continuous painful exercise in avoidance. We would lose our natural lives in an attitude of such denial. We might plunge ahead on the basis of whatever attractive maps we could conjure up in our minds, but we would surely go astray by doing so.

Most of us like to think we're getting somewhere when in fact we don't have a clue as to where our direction is ultimately taking us. Like the Buddha, Yogi doesn't seem to think that being lost is a problem, but rather sees it as a common and unavoidable human circumstance. And while all the rest of us are traveling along at a good clip with routes and destinations in mind, Yogi says, "Hey guys, you know what? We're lost." Most people don't like to hear that because they need to think that they're not lost. But as soon as someone points out the contrary, all directions of travel are exposed as equally arbitrary and uncertain. If, like Yogi, you can appreciate the humor in this comedy of human misdirection, you'll be freed of the necessity to convince yourself that you've got your life's travels under control.

OUR LIVES ARE NOT PATTERNS to be cut out and sewn together like pieces of cloth into a garment of our choosing. Such life patterns are mostly interpolations of arbitrary thought. Like others, I may cling to such a fiction in preference to the obvious uncertainties that are otherwise apparent—and I don't want anyone like Yogi exposing my pretense and thereby undermining the tenuous self-assurance I gain from it. I was backpacking with friends one early spring in the high Sierra well above snowline. We'd left our camp with all our overnight provisions at the margin of a frozen lake and had gone for a walk in the woods. It was toward evening and five of us were wandering about in the deep snow with darkness coming on. With the sun sinking fast, I'm certain that each of us realized that we were lost. But being caught out on the trail with the plunging night temperatures and no way to keep sufficiently warm was a consequence too grave to be admitted. And so for a while we just acted as if we knew where we were going. It's the sort of situation where the sooner you face the fact that you're lost the better your chances are for some sort of reasonable correction.

It isn't just five foolish hikers that are lost, stumbling blindly about in the snow trying to convince themselves that they know where they're going. The collective population of whole nations, indeed virtually that of the whole world, is lost as well. The world is enchanted with what it deems "progress"—and every little "modernization," every technological "advance," every additional "convenience" is seen as evidence that we're really getting somewhere. And all the while our various armies spread bloodshed across the globe in pursuit of economic and strategic advantage, ambitious industries foul the air and water, corporations count their profits, stock prices soar, and we congratulate ourselves on each rise in gross national product. All the statistics of commerce tell us we know what we're doing. In the meantime, the hour of our reckoning grows nearer. The polar ice melts and great gaps in the ozone appear. Vast populations of plants, birds, fish, and animals of all sorts disappear from the earth forever. And all the while we plunge forward, killing one another over the dwindling resources left to us, counting each short-term gain as evidence that we're getting somewhere.

Zen practice, which is to say the practice of life itself, is said to rest on the three supports of great faith, great aspiration, and great doubt. We humans have certainly got the faith, though a tenuous one, a little like whistling hopefully in a darkened woods trying to convince ourselves we're unafraid—and we've got the aspiration as well, demonstrating an unqualified zeal for carrying out our aims no matter how misdirected they might be. But we're not much given to doubt, for the cost of doubt is too great to bear. How can we possibly acknowledge the awful waste we've laid about us? How can we ever bring ourselves to admit that we humans have engaged ourselves in a centuries-long mistake? Yet, everyone knows that a tripod with only two legs will topple.

It's our misfortune that we humans are so readily attracted to constructing of our lives mental maps of linear progression aimed at improvement. We draw false and unwarranted assurance from maintaining a mental file of such maps as evidence that we know where we've been and where we're going. We like to think that what we're doing and where we're headed amounts to making "progress." We refuse to allow for error, and we don't much like chance events either, because they can't be anticipated or planned for and constitute a kind of messy interference in an otherwise well-designed itinerary.

Margaret Simmons, a clerk at Future Foods Corporation, is commuting to work this morning in her new hybrid car. She has this particular day and, in fact, her whole life, pretty well planned out and is assured that things are going well. She'll have lunch at the company cafeteria, which is featuring a new line of "Meal-in-One" offerings. Margaret can get a whole day's nutritional needs from a single cup of fortified yogurt. What will they think of next? Margaret is a great believer that "they" will always think of something. She counts on that; it makes her feel like she knows where she's going. Margaret's running a little late this morning but the traffic's moving well and she feels that she's making pretty good time.

A Vocabulary of Peace

*I*N PRACTICING RIGHT SPEECH, I've tried to do as the Buddha taught and avoid telling lies. I've also worked to refrain from language that slanders others and causes enmity and distrust between people. I've tried as well to avoid rude and abusive language, and to let go of all idle, useless talk and gossip. My success in this has been varied and uncertain. But in the trying, I've become increasingly aware of how the language I speak, the actual words that come out of my mouth, tends to shape my view of the world and determine what I think and what I do. This is probably self-evident, but it's nonetheless a common perception to assume that language is in the service of thought and not the other way around. But once a word has gained currency among a body of speakers, that word feeds back on its inventor, continually reinforcing whatever connotations have attached themselves to the word's common usage. In a certain we way, we truly become what we say—and this has critical implications for the work of the bodhisattva.

As Buddhists, our human work, now as always, is to realize a sane, nonviolent, just, and merciful human society. It is work to be done without apparent assurance of success, but it is not work to be done without preferences. It involves a choice between those who equally include the interests of all beings whoever and wherever they might be and those who are selective, between those who place themselves first and those who would sacrifice themselves to the interest of others when fairness requires it, between those who would rely on military and economic force as a final resort to settle differences and those who would put aside such force and, as a final resort, rely instead on the persuasion of kindness, compassion, and love. And persuasion of this latter sort can only go forward when we truly talk to each other as equals, putting aside all instruments of coercion, as brothers and sisters the world over. This is the talk of "let me be your friend," of "let me understand." It's not a talk we've been getting much practice in as of late. But it's the one conversation that speaks in the vocabulary of the peace that we long for.

The vocabulary of ambition, greed, hatred, and force is quite another thing. It's the sort of vocabulary that disguises its intent in euphemisms like "national interest," one of the cruelest expressions current in the English lexicon. The phrase's capacity for cruelty lies in the narrowness of its application and in the fact that the phrase is so familiar that it goes unquestioned and unexamined. Contend that any policy or action is in our national interest and it's cheerfully assumed to be a good thing. Whether or not it's in anyone else's national interest is not seen as an issue. "If it's good for me, that's what matters." Thus, in the name of national interest, governments the world over suppress, exploit, and threaten other nations, and do so by cultivating their citizens' tacit or explicit consent.

Any dialogue that serves to promote the "national interest" will fail to answer to the world's urgent call for the dignity of a fair and accessible livelihood, for peace and justice and mercy, for a politics and a foreign policy that doesn't insist on putting others last. I'm speaking here of the one value that can redeem our species and set right our long history of greed and violence.

The single complete and encompassing value is the brotherhood and sisterhood of all beings—human, animal, plant, and mineral; sentient and insentient. All other expressions of real value are footnotes to this fundamental truth. It's a truth whose realization requires a continuing dialogue conducted in the language of peace. If we want to speak truly to each other, we must speak as people of one tongue, one mind, one flesh, one human family. It's easy to see how the call for "patriotism," a concept Samuel Johnson defined as the last refuge of a scoundrel, runs counter to universal sisterhood and brotherhood. As Tolstoy once put it, "A patriotic ideal tends to unite people within a designated group to the exclusion of others outside the group. This is true of all patriotic emblems, with its anthems, ceremonies, and monuments, which, while uniting some people, makes that very union a cause of separation between the selected people it unites and all others; so that union of a patriotic kind is often a source not merely of division but even of enmity toward others." "Patriotism" is a word whose currency increases whenever a country's national interest is best served by rallying the population around a common opposition to the "enemy."

Look at any political map and you'll see a world of complex boundaries dividing the earth into separate political jurisdictions—continents into nations, nations into states, states into counties and townships, and on down to the survey lines of the lot on which your house rests. Within each of these subdivisions of the earth's surface, there reside people and governments claiming varying degrees of sovereignty for their portion of the planet. And larger political jurisdictions, such as the United States, claim the right of an absolute sovereignty comprised of complete independence and self-governance to be held inviolable from outside interference of any sort. From this heartless and excluding notion of sovereignty arises a consequent reliance on militarism that has brought the powers of the world to expend their resources not on cultivating the seeds of universal brotherhood and sisterhood but rather on building a preferably unmatched military capability. We must do these things, we are told, in defense of our sovereignty.

"National interest," "patriotism," "sovereignty" are staples of the vocabulary of force. They are instruments of citizen control, designed to cultivate the innocent and gullible attitudes that serve to promote ambitions of unscrupulous intent. But the greatest pity is that such language obscures clarity, tempting its users to seek comfort in terms that disguise their own predilection toward greed and advantage. It's a language that lies to the one who speaks it.

I ask myself what my obligation is to the world and its peoples. The overriding ethic of all Buddhism is *ahimsa* or the practice of non-harming. That means that I'm sworn to live a life free of violence, but by implication I'm also sworn to the cultivation of peace. Is it enough that I live my own life as peacefully as I can or am I called upon to do more? Do my Buddhist vows require me to intervene when violence occurs and encourage peace whenever I can by direct and active means? I obviously can't settle this for anyone else, but my conscience insists that I act on behalf of peace in every way that I can.

What's more, the struggle for a peaceful society is as much a struggle over who controls language as it is over who controls wealth and armaments. You can't wage wars, either economic or military, without the consent of the people. And to get such consent, the vocabulary of ambition, greed, hatred, and force, deceitfully disguised in words of apparent virtue, is broadcast through a vastly expanded media into virtually every neighborhood and home throughout the world. If I am to practice right speech in a way that really counts for something, it's not enough anymore for me to merely watch what *I* say—I must watch what others say as well. I take it as understood that the fulfillment of the bodhisattva vow to save all beings obligates me to counter the manipulative and deceitful language of force wherever it occurs.

Even so, the language of peace already rides our own tongues. We know for ourselves how to say love, to say kindness, forgiveness, mercy, compassion. It's the heart's own sutra written in the blood and failure of centuries of forceful coercion and strife.

How Civilization Is Made

*I*T WAS 1946 AND I WAS FOURTEEN when I opened a thin little book that began with the following description of a moment in the life of a young Japanese woman:

At exactly fifteen minutes past eight in the morning of August 6, 1945, Japanese time, at the moment when the atomic bomb flashed above Hiroshima, Miss Toshiko Sasaki, a clerk in the personnel department of East Asia Tin Works, had just sat down at her plant office and was turning her head to speak to the girl at the next desk.

John Hersey's *Hiroshima* altered for good the direction of my life. Toshiko Sasaki was just about to say something to the girl at the next desk, perhaps a simple morning greeting or a comment on the pretty dress she was wearing or a curiosity about a date she'd gone on the night before—but whatever it was she meant to say, it was never said because before she could speak, the world in which such things might be said was incinerated in a flash of immense heat and blinding light. I became an advocate for peace and for the abolition of war because I was never able to put out of mind all the little ordinary things people were doing in Hiroshima the instant the bomb ended a hundred thousand lives.

I'd known about the bomb for over a year at the time, ever since it had been dropped. And I knew that something terrible had taken place, but it wasn't until I read John Hersey's book that I understood that the dropping of the atomic bomb on Hiroshima and Nagasaki was something that should never have happened to anyone anywhere on the earth. I also somehow knew that the Toshiko Sasaki's of Hiroshima, the clerks and factory workers, housewives and schoolteachers, the nameless "inconsequential" inhabitants of that doomed city, lived lives that counted for everything that constitutes the best of what builds and sustains a genuine, human civilization.

The conventional view of history postulates a civilization that advances on a colossal scale with grand events: the coming to power of great leaders, wars won and lost, the framing of constitutions, the ratification of treaties, the overthrow of governments, the rise and fall of sovereign nations. It's mostly a history of the accumulation of power and the use of force, a chronicle of things built up only to be torn down again, things joined only to be divided once more. There's no question but that these broad historical events exert great influence on human matters. They are the forces that wrench, twist, and dislocate the lives of humans everywhere, but they are not the factors that shape genuine civilization. Civilization is made by households, its economy carried out on the scale of family and friend, its currency an exchange on the level of person to person. It's a quality of kindness in human affairs that sustains what little civilization we can manage. I believe the factors that actually shape civilization are acts so random and ordinary that their significance goes unmarked.

IN THE SOUTHERN CALIFORNIA FARM COUNTRY where I was raised the women put up food for the winter months in the manner they'd learned from their mothers and grandmothers. In my family of five—my mother and father, my brother Rowland, my sister Evelyn, and me—we began the process of canning and storing away food from the moment the garden began to yield in spring until we'd exhausted the last remnants of it in the late fall. All the farm families had a garden and orchard, and not much cash. They either planted and harvested and preserved or they couldn't expect to eat very well when the days shortened and darkened toward winter.

The mornings my mother took the canning pot with its bottle rack from a pantry shelf and hauled it into the kitchen, she would never have thought she was doing anything for anybody but herself and her family. And when she scrubbed the pot clean and filled it with water to boil and went to the garden to pick a basket of string beans, she didn't know such common actions joined with others to sustain whatever sense and decency the world is capable of. She would never have presumed that the rows of jars, neatly labeled and dated, lining the pantry shelves of a winter afternoon, were the orderly makings of a civilization. Yet it is these numberless little acts, this uncalculated responsiveness to the needs of the moment, more than all the dictates of empires and presidencies, that draws us into common community.

We do it best when we don't know we're doing it at all. Wiping a kid's runny nose or sticking a thermometer under a sick child's tongue are actions taken without self-consciousness of any sort. When I see my townspeople hanging out the wash or raking fall leaves or setting the table for the evening meal or jogging behind a child snuggled up in an infant carrier in the town park, I know that I am witnessing exactly those forces that counteract the divisive ambitions of military and corporate aims.

Civilization only asks of us that we live kindly and now. We are wise beyond our knowing when we do so. It's not policy or ideology that makes us neighbors; it's not the defense of state sovereignty or "national interest" that sustains communities. It's much more a kitchen and yard thing, an elementary school and town park thing, in which we are watchful of one another.

WHEN THE JENSEN FAMILY had need of more farm acreage and leased a farm further out of town, the contents of the kitchen pantry with all its canned goods moved with us. But in the moving, we inadvertently loosened the seal on a jar of string beans. And when Mother, failing to notice this, served them for Sunday afternoon dinner, we were made desperately sick as a consequence. We were all of us so dazed and debilitated by the sudden effects of food poisoning that we were unable to help each other—except my baby sister, Evelyn, who was only a year old at the time and hadn't eaten any of the beans. Neither Mother nor Father could even make it to the phone to call for help. We crawled into the bathroom and lay on the floor with the ceiling and walls swimming about us, and when one of us had to retch we dragged ourselves onto the rim of the toilet to throw up, and Mother, lying where she was, could just reach the toilet chain to flush.

Gradually night came on and the house grew dark. I think it was Mother who took my hand in hers first. I was able to reach my brother with the free hand, and he took Father's, and Father reached back to Mother. And Evelyn crawled around and over us, supposing, I guess, that it was some sort of game. My mind hovers now above that old farmhouse where it lay surrounded by dusty fields. I see the four of us there on the bathroom floor, a sprawl of stricken flesh, legs and arms askew, joined hand to hand, on a background of faded linoleum.

Struggles of ambition and fear characterize the grand enterprises that populate the pages of what passes for the history of civilization. They are the forces that threaten to strike down everything that is good about us. The may kill us some day. But a single family that remembers to join hands will by small effects sustain kindness and generosity until the very end.

Eventually Mother recovered enough to reach the phone and call Dr. Robbins from his bed to come to our aid. He came, yawning, in the middle of the night, bearing the instruments of diagnosis and treatment he'd been given by his predecessor. He managed to get each of us into bed, and he found something in the kitchen to feed Evelyn and left her asleep in her crib. He said with a twinkle that he could positively assure us we wouldn't die but that we'd be a few days recovering, and would Mother like him to call our neighbor, Mrs. Reeder, to come by in the morning and give a hand.

Later Mother cried at having to dispose of the jars of string beans she'd worked so hard to put away for the winter, her heart responding to a small error that might have cost her children and husband their lives. She would have cried equally for any family whose economy and lives were threatened by such a mistake. We were in the midst of World War II and Mother would sometimes cry over the radio news. She was never an activist, nor was she one with a conscious mission of any sort. She was too busy making life happen to notice that civilization was flowering in her own kitchen. I followed her one morning to the garden, which lay fallow now, and watched her unscrew the lids of the bean jars and dump the contents onto the compost heap. And when she saw me there, she mopped her eyes dry on her apron and put me to work helping her.

MR. MUJAKU AND HIS WIFE had an agreement to meet at a certain fountain in a square in Hiroshima in the event that their house was destroyed in an air raid. Mr. Mujaku was at work on the outskirts of Hiroshima when the bomb exploded and Mrs. Mujaku was at home. They both survived the initial blast, but their house was left leaning precariously and the whole neighborhood was being consumed in sudden flames. Mr. Mujaku, realizing how extensive the destruction of the city had been, left work in search of his wife. Finding their house and neighborhood in flames and not knowing if his wife was even alive, he went to the fountain where they'd agreed to meet. He found her waiting for him there. She'd rescued a few biscuits and some tea from the house before it caught fire. And while Hiroshima lay in waste about them and their very bodies hummed with the lethal radiation that would one day take their lives from them, Mr. and Mrs. Mujaku, in a saving gesture beyond the power of any bomb, sat on a bench by the fountain and drank their tea and ate their biscuits as they'd always done.

Hot and Cold

THERE ARE LARGE AND IMPERSONAL FORCES operating upon our lives that pretty much determine where our travels take us and what happens to us at any given time. I don't always like the circumstances I'm given and would prefer something else—but I've noticed that my complaints about this have roughly the same effect as complaining about the weather. I've never persuaded the rain to let up just because I wanted sunshine. The life I get isn't something I can simply choose to have or not have, and wishing it to be otherwise is useless.

It's precisely this pointless resistance to circumstance that comes to bear upon the Buddha's teaching of the Middle Way, a teaching popularly viewed as instruction in holding a position mid-way between opposites. Drawing on his own experience, the Buddha warned against both self-indulgence and self-denial, saying, "One should not pursue sensual pleasure, which is low, vulgar, coarse, ignoble, and unbeneficial, and should not pursue self-mortification, which is painful, ignoble, and unbeneficial." To this end, he encouraged moderation in all things and advised his followers "to restrain their senses and to avoid looking at forms around them with either feelings of aversion or attraction."

The problem with this is that one can't really avoid aversion and attraction by simple restraint of the senses. If I'm trying to restrain my senses, it's because I'm attracted to such restraint and averse to the lack of it, which means that I've only shifted the object of my affection from one attraction to another. What's more, it's hard work to try and convince myself not to take pleasure in something I take pleasure in. If a butterfly or a sunset or a line of poetry strikes me with a sense of pleasure, if I take delight in these things, how am I to teach myself *not* to delight in them?

Nonetheless, students of Buddhism seeking the Middle Way often end up trying to do just that. In their avoidance of attraction and aversion, they struggle to get through the day without either of these responses and end up in a preposterous attempt to not feel too good or too bad or to not have too much or too little fun. It's a practice in cultivating an unruffled composure, a "flat affect," posing as inherent moderation. Anything that excites one too much (or too little?) is seen as detrimental. Followers of the Middle Way who behave like this tend to speak reverently of "non-attachment" and "equanimity," revealing a sad (and sometimes also comic) yet always costly confusion regarding the terms. Since attraction and aversion are one and the same, so that you can never get one without the other, resistance of any sort can't be taken to define either non-attachment or equanimity. The idea of the Middle Way as a safely negotiated route between resisted polarities is a crude duality of human thought.

Zen has a quite different take on this:

A monk asked Tung-shan, "When cold and heat come, how can we avoid them?"

Tung-shan said, "Why don't you go to the place where there is no cold or heat?"

The monk said, "What is the place where there is no cold or heat?"

Tung-shan said, "When it's cold, the cold kills you; when it's hot, the heat kills you."

The monk wants to know how to avoid the mental tyranny of opposites that compels a reaction relative to one or the other extreme of some polarity. He wants to know how to obtain release from the *either/or* mind that's always confronted with a choice between *this* or *that*. Perhaps he thinks he could accomplish this by positioning himself somewhere in the middle where contrary forces would conveniently neutralize themselves by virtue of equal opposition. Or maybe he thinks there's a way to altogether do away with opposite forces by simply ignoring or rejecting the alternatives they seem to offer. Tung-shan is telling him that whatever comes to him let it be wholly and completely itself without reference to an alternative. If heat comes, just be hot. If cold comes, just be cold.

Hot and cold function as opposing alternatives only when they're brought into the mind as comparative options. As strange as it may seem, Buddhist equanimity is achieved not by trying to position oneself midway between extremes but rather by allowing things to be as they are, extreme or not. All preference is in opposition to something, and it is this selectivity that puts us at odds with the moment and results in lives that are habitually out of kilter.

When a monk came to Zen Master Chao-chou looking for a point of reference that would distinguish meditation from other lesser states of mind, Chao-chou turned his request aside:

A monk asked Chao-chou, "What is meditation?"

Chao-chou said, "Non-meditation."

"How can meditation be non-meditation?" the monk asked.

Chao-chou said, "It's alive! It's alive!"

The mind of meditation has no distinguishing differentiae because it is wholly inclusive and thus free from the restraint to accord with any particular point of reference. The mind of meditation is an ordinary mind, a natural mind, too alive to be constrained within contrived limits. Ordinary mind doesn't *abstract* concepts from reality because it *is* reality and can't be contained within any of the various philosophies I might invent. It is wholly unresponsive to the best of my schemes. Ordinary mind is hot and cold, wet and dry, large and small, coarse and fine. It is all of these things. Ordinary mind forfeits nothing of itself to fear or restraint. It makes no accommodation to caution or comfort. It's alive. If I'm concerned to avoid opposites, I'll only end up avoiding life itself.

And while I struggle to moderate or equalize the forces that play upon my being, hot and cold will remain just as they are—actual and unavoidable.

Impermanence

A PRIMARY TENET OF BUDDHISM is the reality of impermanence. Often the upshot of this teaching is presented as "nothing ever stays the same." This is fine enough so far as it goes, but I would add that nothing ever *is* the same, never *is* what you think it is. It's not merely that everything is subject to change and that the changes occur more swiftly and capriciously than can be captured in thought, and it's not only that our perceptions are bound to be mistaken in one way or another because they're always out of date, rather it's that thought itself is selective and thus at best only a partial sampling of what's really going on. No one who is the least bit mindful of his surroundings need ever be put to "meditating on" impermanence. Impermanence is all there is, inclusive of the mind that meditates. If I'm paying attention at all, my whole natural life is a meditation on impermanence.

I've trained under both Soto and Rinzai teachers, and in neither of these Zen traditions have I ever been set to the task of meditating on the impermanence of anything. What I have been set to do is to notice what's going on around me. When I give this sort of curious attention a try, I'm surprised at how unfamiliar the neighborhood is. This fresh strangeness is the gift of attention. When an object appears familiar, it's a certainty that I'm merely seeing my *idea* of the object rather than the object itself.

Furthermore, the idea I form of an object is invariably a "rounding off" of the object to accommodate a categorical generalization, whereas the object itself is always sharp, specific to this exact moment, and doesn't repeat itself. Categorical generalizations render *actual* objects, persons, and events into *types* of objects, persons, and events. There are in reality no such types, but only the discrete things themselves. The perception of an apparent continuity of identity in an object is merely a story we tell ourselves, and the best of our stories quickly grow stale and predictable. Fixed thoughts of this sort isolate and confine the mind to the familiar, weary, habitual conversation I carry on with myself. Freedom consists of not having that conversation, and that's why impermanence is so liberating. Freedom arrives when I don't know what to make of the world, and thus make nothing of it at all.

Traditional Buddhist teaching cites impermanence as a source of human suffering. The sense of this is easily apparent when we acknowledge that among the changes we can expect to experience in our lives are those of sickness, old age, and death. And of course, there are all sorts of other random and accidental occurrences that involve change and loss—we lose our jobs, our partners, our waistlines, hair, teeth. The house burns down or the mortgage company forecloses. Our car gets totaled or stolen or repossessed. Our daughters and sons who were once so sweet and compliant have lately taken to sassing us.

It's easy to perceive impermanence as a whole lot of trouble—

but the interesting twist that's frequently overlooked is that impermanence is only a problem when it's perceived as such. The Buddha was quite clear about this in his formulation of the Four Noble Truths wherein he cited the *resistance* to impermanence and not impermanence itself as the source of suffering. Clinging, he said, is suffering. So, if, in the face of inevitable change, I try to hold on to any preferred situation, I'm certain to suffer when the situation is altered. In fact, I suffer whether alteration occurs or not, because clinging is itself a tense and guarded defense against the threat of change.

What's rarely acknowledged or even recognized in the traditional Buddhist teaching on impermanence is the *joy* that accompanies impermanence. If we look upon impermanence as merely an inconvenience to be borne as graciously as possible, then the best we can hope for is to neutralize the negative effects of change. But impermanence doesn't take sides, and change can lead to all sorts of consequences including those of sheer delight. Perhaps the notable absence in Buddhist literature of any popular affirmation of impermanence is a consequence of no one feeling a need to point out the obvious. Yet in the absence of any such affirmation, impermanence is often perceived in rather grim terms as something that must be endured without complaint. It's a viewpoint that reduces equanimity to a state of merely not expecting too much in order to avoid disappointment. It's a little like tiptoeing past potential trouble while holding your breath.

If I don't insist on defining impermanence as unsatisfactory, then it's quite natural, indeed unavoidable, to celebrate impermanence. We do it all the time. The sun rises, only to set and then rise again. Water falls from the skies and flows down rivers to the sea where it rises once more to the sky. Just a moment's pause to consider the passing of the seasons is enough to convince anyone that not only is impermanence the source of all possible *joy* in this life but that impermanence is the *movement* of life itself. I must breathe out in order to breathe in. And in the same way, even death invites new pleasures into the world. When the widow who lived on the corner of East Sacramento Avenue and Laburnum passed away, a young couple moved in to restore the house and raise two daughters. Here on this finite planet, each of our deaths gives way to the lives of others. It's obvious to me that I must relinquish the space I occupy, the air I breathe, all those resources needed to support my continuation, if my grandchildren and your grandchildren are to have space and air and resources of their own.

That death is essential to birth and that the old must die for the sake of the young is not a thought that will necessarily reconcile me to the death of a child. For in such a circumstance, I will surely feel that chance has made a mistake in taking the life of the child and not my own. But even then, only change can deliver me from my sorrow, and if I ever manage to smile again it will be by the blessing of impermanence.

For all its potential sorrows and misfortunes, life is, after all, the only pleasure available. And "life" is just a collective term for the movement the universe makes, which is to say life is the manifestation of impermanence. Even solid rock, in its apparent impenetrable fixity, gradually disperses toward delight. If it did not, there'd be no soil, no flower, no pollinating insect, no grazing or browsing animal or bird or human. Whatever delight you and I have ever experienced is the gift of broken rock.

We do well to remember that and pay homage to the forces of impermanence.

Kelp

IT'S SAID THAT THE BUDDHIST PATH is one of resolving the "great matter of birth and death." But what insight could possibly be found or action taken that resolves the apparent conflict between such seemingly irreconcilable poles of one's life? Is there some discoverable truth that puts the matter to rest, and what, if anything, do I know about such a truth? If Buddhism has an insight into this, I don't think it's exclusive to Buddhists. I think we all know something firsthand that crosses the gulf between life and death, some sense or intuition that joins our coming into existence with our apparent going out. Let me tell you of an event that took place long before I had any notion of what Buddhist thought and practice entailed.

I WAS SEVENTEEN and I was spear fishing one mid-October morning under a great floating kelp forest in the deep waters off the Laguna Beach coast in Southern California. It was a windy morning with spray blown back off the tips of the cresting waves where they rolled into the beach under a bright sun. I was pushing myself down among the swaying columns of bunched kelp stems that anchored the undulating canopy to the sea floor in pursuit of a large fish, a cabazone I'd spotted sliding over the face of a rock below. And then everything turned dark, and I knew that the kelp had closed in on me overhead.

I rose back toward the surface looking for a spot where a little light leaked through the kelp, marking an opening in the thick canopy overhead. I was unconcerned because I'd always before found a space through which to surface—but now I could find none, and I was running out of time. I tugged at the dark floating mass of matted kelp leaves and stems, trying to thread my way to the surface. But I only succeeded in entangling myself and had to struggle to get free. And of course I was running out of breath—I knew that in a few seconds I'd breathe water into my lungs. There simply was no escape! Struggle was useless and with death assured, I simply gave in to that reality and let myself sink toward the ocean floor. And in the instant before chance opened a slim channel in the canopy and a shaft of light lit up the back of my hand and I surfaced into a sparkling sun, something surprising and marvelous happened.

It was like this. There was only a dark drifting downward. Under the spreading kelp forest, the sea was wondrously silent. Somewhere above, the wind pushed waves onto the beach, and fields of alfalfa and lima beans and orange orchards stretched across Orange County, and the women on the farms hung out laundry to dry, and a seventeen-year-old boy was drowning off the coast at Laguna Beach. I saw everyone and everything I'd ever known, and all were drifting with me to the floor of the sea. And nothing was lost because, knowing I was to die, an absolute poverty of preference prevailed in me and I was freed from the tug of hopeful expectations. With no future left me, I was intensely given to exactly what was happening without reserve or option of any sort. It was utterly and completely peaceful.

Now, don't assume I wanted to die. When the kelp parted, I was glad to reach the surface alive. But nonetheless the universe had offered me something I could not have thought to ask for. It was something of an insight into the reality where birth and death are just movements in the one and only life. In those dark seconds when I was certain of dying, I felt an ease like that of a wave break-ing, throwing itself on the sand, knowing itself in its momentary dissolution to be inseparable from the body of the sea to which it would be drawn back once again. And there under the kelp, I too was drawn out of myself into the lives of all that I knew; I couldn't really say what, if anything, would die when my lungs would fill with water.

An old Chinese story is very pointed on this particular matter:

Tao-wu and Chien-yuan went to a house to make a condo-lence call. Yuan hit the coffin and said, "Alive or dead?" Wu said, "I won't say alive, and I won't say dead." Yuan said, "Why won't you say?" Wu said, "I won't say." Halfway back, as they were returning, Yuan said, "Tell me right away, Teacher; if you don't tell me, I'll hit you." Wu said, "You may hit me, but I won't say." Yuan then hit him.

Later Tao-wu passed on. Yuan went to Shih-shuang and brought up the foregoing story. Shuang said, "I won't say alive, and I won't say dead." Yuan said, "Why won't you say?" Shuang said, "I won't say, I won't say." At these words Yuan had an insight.

I don't know what Chien-yuan's insight was, but I like to think he realized that the opposition we imagine to exist between life and death is a mistaken perception. We think the two are separate; we imagine life begins at birth and that death overtakes life at some future time. But life and death are continuous. The quick and the dead are like the rhythmic ebb and flow of the sea's tide, a timeless movement of one body of water. When I look at things in this way, I realize that even my individual birth and death are not really my own, but simply alternating phases of the greater life I share.

The repeated reference one finds in Buddhism to resolving "the great matter of birth and death" speaks a language that makes the whole thing sound a little too grand and remote somehow. And while the phrase may very well point to a crucial awakening in a student's pursuit of the Way, I don't think it's a perception that's extraordinary. I think it's more a matter of simplicity than anything else, a freedom from worried spiritual elaboration. Life doesn't require you to make a project out of resolving anything. And you don't have to be brought to the verge of drowning or barely escape being run down by a speeding vehicle or told you're dying from a terminal disease or any such extremity in order to realize your place in birth and death. You just have to notice where you are and what you are, and this can happen to you at any time—and probably has done so frequently.

Maybe you didn't notice at the time—but if you recall now, do you remember the blooming hibiscus swarming with bees or the kid with the freckles laughing in the rain or the newborn infant's cry or the gulls riding the wind above the sea? Do you remember how these things drew you out of yourself? Do you remember how vast and deep the water is?

Mother Earth

MOTHER EARTH is a metaphor so embedded in common usage that I might wager it is the one English language cliché most likely to outlast all possible change. But a metaphorical cliché persists for a reason, and the reason is that the metaphor embodies an indispensable truth. People repeat the same combination of words over and over through the centuries not because they can't think of anything else to say but because the words fit the living fact of their lives. "Mother Earth" is like that.

A *human* mother nurtures and protects within her own body the developing embryo of the infant she will deliver into the care of the *earth* mother at the moment of birth. A human mother is a surrogate mother as it were, both she and her infant sustained in her pregnancy by the mother of us all. In giving birth, she only gives back to earth what belongs to earth. The child at her breast draws sustenance from the one and only source available to any of us. We are all like nursing infants, utterly dependent upon the earth to bring us forth, not once only but every instant of our lives. It is the earth that gives and sustains life, and to think otherwise is a fanatical and prideful arrogance. Chinese philosophy has a view quite unlike the otherworldliness of Western Biblical traditions. In the Chinese view, we humans occupy a place between heaven and earth that partakes equally of both. We sit, stand, and walk upon the surface of the earth with the great canopy of the heavens spread above. The prevailing idea is that we humans are comprised inseparably of both spirit and matter. An interesting divergence from typical Western thought is that in the Chinese world the earth does not ascend to the heavens but rather the heavens descend to earth. Humans, occupying the link between heaven and earth, do not abandon the earth in order to rise to the realm of the spirit. Instead spirit makes its home in the very body of living matter.

If we humans neglect our earthly ties in favor of more "spiritual" aspirations, we will have lost the vital connection between spirit and the immediacy of flesh and all matter. Being a Buddhist, I spend hours sitting nearer the ground than most. The sitting is an enactment of the return to the source, a daily pilgrimage I've come to trust beyond any other travels I might undertake, and without which my most elevated thoughts are merely groundless abstractions wherein the spirit withers in sterile isolation.

Age has a way of calming even the most ardent spiritual zeal. Our last years are more a thing of the valley than one of the heights. It's as if a debt we owe has come due, and the earth that loaned us life prepares to take us back in payment. It's a wise and humbling economy understood by the old. In the tale of the Pardoner from Chaucer's *Canterbury Tales*, a wizened and bent man is walking along a country road. A group of young partygoers spy him coming up the trail leaning on his staff and chide him for being so ancient. Why, they want to know, does he go on like this when he's too old for girls or partying or getting any fun from life? Why doesn't he give up when he's so old he can barely hold himself upright? In their youth, they think perhaps that they can have life on their own terms, party when they want and die when they want. But the old man knows his circumstance better than they, and remembers what gives life and what waits to receive it back, what gives breath and what will ultimately take the last breath home to itself. He tells the young partygoers that he has long been ready to die. "I walk on like this day after day tapping the earth with my staff, calling, 'Mother, let me in! Mother, let me in!'"

The partygoers are glad to party when they can. To that extent my heart goes out to them and I'm happy for them in their youthful innocence. But when they chide old age, their arrogance and bluster only serves to mask their deeper fears, not fears of death alone but of life as well. In their willful play they purchase a momentary forgetfulness, and for a few minutes or hours they are their own persons serving their own needs, blessedly unaware that every breath drawn and every pulse of blood that courses its way through their veins is given them by the earth mother of us all, over which they hold no sway whatsoever. It is this moment-by-moment indebtedness to forces beyond us that we humans so often find hard, even bitter, to admit.

We fancy ourselves independent, living in an absolutely fictional autonomy. Yet our bodies know, even when we don't, that we are nothing but what Mother Earth herself deems us to be. We are creatures born of dirt and leaf, and wind and rain and sunlight, and it is these forces that hold us in life at this very moment. We would do well in our travels to tap the earth from time to time as Chaucer's old man does. Or at the very least touch a hand to the earth, not so much beseeching entry whose time may have not yet come, but in prayerful gratitude for the ongoing gift of life.

Impression Management

IMPRESSION MANAGEMENT is an effort to control what others think of you. It consists of persuading others to acknowledge you in the same terms as you acknowledge yourself. If you're caught up in impression management, you're forever at pains to secure a favorable public "image" of yourself. And when others see you in less favorable terms, it becomes an offense and threat to your person. Impression management never works, but nonetheless individuals will exhaust themselves in the effort to make it work, and nations will readily go to war in the vain effort of forcing the world to submit to their self-admiring prejudice. Since you can't really control how others choose to see you, it should be easy to understand how marketing your personal identity forfeits self-regard and puts you at the disposal of others.

An intriguing story involving Zen Master Hakuin shows how to free yourself from this bind:

A beautiful girl in the village turned up pregnant and when her angry parents demanded to know who the father was, she accused Hakuin the Zen monk who lived in a nearby hut and whom everyone revered as living a life without blame. When the parents confronted Hakuin with the daughter's accusation, Hakuin simply replied, "Is that so?"

The people of the village, accepting Hakuin's guilt, now viewed him as a hypocrite and religious imposter. Hakuin calmly endured this criticism of himself, and when the parents brought him the newborn baby, demanding that he take care of it since it was his responsibility, Hakuin simply said, "Is that so?" and took the baby into his keeping.

For months he took care of the child until the daughter could no longer bear the lie she'd told, and confessed that a young man in the village was actually the father. The parents rushed to Hakuin's hut to take back the baby and apologize for their false opinion of him. When they explained what had happened, Hakuin merely said, "Is that so?" as he handed the child over to them.

Hakuin understood clearly the futility of arguing with what the world chose to think of him, and kept his own counsel in that regard. Instead of vainly protesting the injustice of the accusation, he simply accommodated himself to the reality at hand, a response that put him in harmony with the moment rather than at odds with it. We may not want our reputation unjustly tarnished nor to be burdened with an obligation not of our own making, but if that's what's happening, there's no use pretending otherwise. It's not that one can't work to change circumstance; it's just that the one freedom that rises above any public impression we might ever hope to make is the freedom to be what we are and act on our own sense of the moment.

Impression management is a kind of lie we tell ourselves for the benefit of others. Among the Buddha's teachings on right speech is the admonition against lying. He asks, "What now is right speech?" And then he answers by saying, "There, someone avoids lying, and abstains from it. He speaks the truth, is devoted to the truth, reliable, worthy of confidence, is not a deceiver of men." To this I would want to add that among the men not to be deceived is the liar himself. One of the grave consequences of depending on lies is that you come to believe them, a consequence fatal to the pursuit of the truth. You can never come to know the world as it is or yourself as you are, so long as you indulge in falsehood. Impression management, with its hopeful falsehoods, is particularly alluring in this respect, a subtle enticement to substitute an impression of oneself more favorable than reality would warrant. Because it's consciously manipulative, impression management is a form of lying that undermines the capacity for genuine self-knowledge. The Buddha goes on to say that the person of right speech, "never knowingly speaks a lie, neither for the sake of his own advantage, nor for the sake of another person's advantage, nor for the sake of any advantage whatsoever." The corrupting falsehood that lies at the heart of every effort to control the impression one makes on another is that it is a behavior undertaken for the sake of advantage.

It's not my business what others think of me. I have no cause to interfere with someone else's impression. When I can rid myself of the urge to manipulate public regard or the lack of it, I turn toward an unprecedented personal freedom. But the really crucial turning comes with the realization that it's not my business what *I* think of me. Without self-regard, the world appears and I can see it as it is.

It was this freedom from self-regard that Zen Master Dogen acknowledged in a famous passage of the *Genjo Koan* (as translated by Kaz Tanahashi):

To study the Buddha Way is to study is to study the self. To study the self is to forget the self. To forget the self is to be actualized by the myriad things. When actualized by myriad things, your body and mind as well as the bodies and minds of others drop away. No trace of realization remains, and this no-trace continues endlessly.

The greatest blessing I'm ever likely to receive is that of forgetting myself, relieved at least for a while from all the worry about what others think of me or what I think of me. For a time there's no one bearing my name whose reputation requires management of any sort. When the person I imagine myself to be is out of the way, I can tend to what's left, and what's left is the whole bright and various world. And with no individual esteem at risk, I can mingle with others in the most natural and unconcerned way. I can do this because I'm no longer distinguishable from the "myriad things." Dogen makes this very point when he insists that studying the Buddha Way is studying the self, acknowledging that the self is all there is, that the self *is* the myriad things.

When I realize that I'm inseparable from all things, I enter a world in which you and I and all things are realized in and of themselves, a world where no one's left to be caught up in impression of any sort.

Washing Bowls

AMONG THE FORTY-EIGHT KOANS recorded in the *Gateless Barrier* is an exchange so simple that one might pass easily by it, were it not that its very simplicity draws to it a certain curiosity and wonderment:

> A monk said to Chao-chou, "I have just entered this monastery. Please teach me."
>
> Chao-chou said, "Have you eaten your rice gruel?"
>
> The monk said, "Yes, I have."
>
> Chao-chou said, "Wash your bowl." The monk understood.

Chao-chou is a late eighth-century Chinese Zen master who lived well into the ninth century, dying at a remarkable age of 120 years. Several of his dialogues with students have been recorded in various koan collections and subsequently annotated and interpreted by later teachers right down to the present time. This particular conversation between Chao-chou and a monk is purportedly given just as it took place, with the exception of the comment that "the monk understood," which is editorial. I don't know what the monk understood or how anyone other than the monk could claim to know that there was any understanding at all.

After all, washing a bowl is not something you understand but rather something you do. The problem for me with the claim that the monk "understood" is that it leads to speculation about *what* the monk understood, and this in turn encourages interpretations that attribute meaning to the dialogue in such a way that a simple line like "Have you eaten your rice gruel?" is rendered as a metaphorical equivalent to "What is the state of your enlightenment?" And from this it follows that the monk's "Yes, I have." means something like "Yes, I'm enlightened." instead of simply, "Yes, I've had breakfast." And the worst of all, and the place where I depart from all such interpretation, is when Chao-chou's "Wash your bowl." is read as an instruction in purification, urging the monk to rid himself of the pride of enlightenment.

I was fortunate to train for a few years with one of the best koan masters I'm ever likely to meet. He would set me to working on a particular koan and, when I came to offer him my response, he never allowed me to explain how I'd arrived at such a response, cutting off explanations of any sort. While I was often anxious to convey to him what "meaning" I'd derived from the koan, he saw no meaning there at all and judged the whole notion of such meaning as extraneous to the purpose at hand. Nothing in his world stood for something else. A thing or event didn't "mean" something; it was just what it was in and of itself. In his work with me, this koan master beat down every attempt of mine to make meaning out of Chao-chou's telling the monk to "Wash your bowl." What did Chao-chou mean "Wash your bowl"? he demanded, challenging me to name whatever meaning

I'd claimed to find there. In the end, there was no meaning, and "Wash your bowl." was all I could ever make of it. My journey with this teacher was loosening my hold on the necessity to attribute meaning and explanation to the facts of my life.

To attribute meaning to an event or to a lifetime of events is an expression of dissatisfaction with things as they are. This is true of even the subtlest attribution. If I wash dishes as a practice in Zen mindfulness, I indulge my resistance to simply washing them in order to get them clean. I want the washing to be more significant than I think it to be, and so make a spiritual project of it. We want our lives to have meaning, and we complain inwardly and sometimes outwardly as well if what we do and what we are appear meaningless. Well, our lives *are* meaningless in any sense of their constituting a meaningful narrative plot of some sort, and when we strain to make them otherwise, we're merely indulging a story we like to tell ourselves. You and I don't manifest in the universe as *meaning*, we manifest as living human beings. We're not here to represent something else. We're here in our own right. A human being, or a sink full of soapy dishes for that matter, is complete in itself without the aid of fictional enhancement.

Still, the monk asked to be taught and unless we are to assume that Chao-chou ignored the request, then Chao-chou's "Wash your bowl." was a teaching. If so, it was a teaching in reduction, and Chao-chou, in turning the monk back toward his own natural life, was showing him that everything he might ever want to know or be was already present in his person, nothing hidden from view. I've had lots of occasions when the person I wanted to be or thought I ought to be was missing somehow—which is just another way to say that I was dissatisfied with who I was and what I was doing. These were times when life didn't add up to my expectations. I was hit with a spell of such misgivings when I was asked by my Soto teachers to found a sangha in my hometown and was first set to teaching Zen. I'd taught college literature and writing for thirty years at the time, but there seemed such a mystique surrounding the function of a Zen teacher that I took it on as a sort of role I was required to fulfill. I couldn't seem to simply show up in my own person and do what was asked of me. I imagined instead that I had to be a distinctly different sort of person to succeed at it. And when I began to teach and the sangha quickly swelled to three times its anticipated attendance, my sense of inadequacy grew with the increased numbers. At times I was profoundly beset with the doubt that I had any qualifications at all to teach Zen and felt fraudulent and utterly lacking in spiritual significance. I see now that the fact that I doubted wasn't a problem. The problem was that I thought I *shouldn't* doubt. I thought that a Zen teacher should know what he was doing without any of the uncertainties I was experiencing. I ought to be different than I was. I ought to be better.

Arguing with myself in this way came in time to feel somehow unkind and ungenerous. And trying to improve myself turned out to be just about as effective as trying to improve the shape of my ears. And the reason for that seemed to be that I was starting from the wrong end of things. Satisfaction has its genesis in acceptance rather than resistance; it's more a matter of noticing what's right than one of noticing what's wrong. Regardless of what I might prefer, this is who I am and this is my world. It is only from this exact person in this exact place that I can step forward into the next moment. It's cranky of me to complain about talents and circumstances. So I've quit trying to size myself up in quite that intentional way. And I find that if I don't insist otherwise I naturally move along with events in their native progression.

Like Chao-chou's monk, there's nothing I need to be taught in order to be who I am. I couldn't even think, let alone say, such a thing before, nor trust the truth of it. To do so would have felt like an expression of the worst kind of self-satisfied hubris, a smug sense of undeserved accomplishment. I hadn't yet learned the humility required to accept myself as I am. I hadn't touched the deeper wonder of receiving the gift of life and the debt of gratitude I owe for it.

When I remember these things, I quit fussing over myself and my situation. I just wash my bowl whenever it needs it, and leave it at that.

Falling to Flat Ground

STUDENTS OF MINE often come to me with a longing for something other than what they've got. They're searching for holier ground than the ground under their feet, a spiritual home other than the one they already inhabit. The old Zen tales are rich with discouragements regarding such searches.

> Ch'ang-ch'ing and Pao-fu were wandering in the hills. Pao-fu pointed to the spot where they were standing and said, "Right here is the top of Mount Sumeru."
> Ch'ang-ch'ing said, "Yes, that's true, but a pity."

Mount Sumeru is the Buddhist equivalent of the ancient Greek's Mount Olympus or maybe the Christian heaven, though Sumeru is taken by Buddhists as figurative rather than literal. Pao-fu is saying that Mount Sumeru is everywhere, that all locations are equally sacred. Ch'ang-ch'ing's wry commentary that that's a pity is in sweet sympathy with our human reluctance to recognize that there's nothing more spiritually significant than what we already have in hand. Ch'ang-ch'ing might have intended as well to point out that it's a pity to call upon the name of Mount Sumeru to enhance the significance of the patch of dirt the two of them were standing on.

Robert Aitken couples the exchange between Pao-fu and Ch'ang-ch'ing with the following exchange between a monk and Chao-chou:

> A monk asked Chao-chou, "What is the lone summit of Mount Sumeru?"
>
> Chao-chou said, "I won't answer that question of yours."
>
> The monk asked, "Why won't you answer my question?"
>
> Chao-chou said, "I'm afraid that if I answered you, you would fall to flat ground."

When I came upon this exchange it was like finding a joke to tell on myself. I think of the times I longed for spiritual experiences while the ones I was having went unacknowledged, or the longing to visit sacred sites while walking on the very temple of the common earth. Chao-chou teases the monk with the prospect of an inevitable fall. And the monk won't have far to fall because the lone summit he fancies is actually one and the same with the flattest ground. He'll discover the truth of that when the heights he anticipates fail to materialize.

I once learned something of the sanctity of flat ground years before I discovered its expression in Zen literature. When I was a boy, my father, a Danish immigrant, was struggling in the wake of the Great Depression to make a farm pay off. He raised turkeys, and by the time of my eighth birthday I was put to work in the fields, spending all the hours I could spare from my schooling at various tasks that my father couldn't attend to because our family's needs required that he hold an outside job. In time the turkeys numbered in the thousands, spread out over 180 acres of leased ground, milling about in fenced enclosures that were trampled to a fine powder laden with manure and buzzing flies. I worked mostly alone, and the sweat and dirt of this place was all I had of Mount Sumeru. If I were to ever find sacred ground, these dusty acres would have to do. In the winter months, the days would darken toward night and lights would appear in the farmhouse windows where mother was cooking a supper that awaited me when my chores were done and I could go to the house myself.

I didn't always work alone. Sometimes when more help was needed, Father would pay Pastor Rawlings to give a hand. Pastor Rawlings was the Pentecostal preacher of a tiny congregation that met in the back room of Birkoff's feed store in Santa Ana Gardens. He was as poor as any of us and, like Father, needed extra work to keep his church going. The pastor was intent on converting me. He thought it would be a "glory in heaven to have a Jensen join the fold." I suspect he calculated that if he could hook me, he might get to other members of the family as well. Whenever we worked together, he went after me with all the instruments of persuasion at his disposal.

All my religious exposure at the time consisted of Sunday services at Trinity Episcopal Church under the guidance of Reverend Hailwood, who wore long white and gold robes and who spoke from an elevated pulpit where he was framed by towering stained glass windows. Pastor Rawlings, in his coveralls and straw hat, shoveling turkey manure into a wagon, didn't look like anything I associated with church. Yet his faith in his mission was as strong and uncompromised as I'm ever likely to see. He was always after me to get right down on my knees with him to pray for deliverance. One day when I complained of the unlikely circumstances of praying in a turkey yard instead of in a church, he told me to put my shovel down, which I did. He took me by the shoulders then and turned me to face him. "We'll make our church right here, son," he said. "Do you think the Lord won't hear us because our knees are in the dirt?" And then he got right down on the ground with his knees in the dust and manure and drifting feathers. I hesitated, but seeing Pastor Rawlings there in the dirt with flies crawling on his hat and his hands clasped together and his head bent forward in prayer, I couldn't resist, and did the same myself. And he prayed for me and told me some things to say for myself. I liked doing it with him, and felt a little less lonely after that.

I don't know whether or not you can call what happened that day a conversion or not, but Pastor Rawlings had shown me that church was wherever I happened to be. After that time of kneeling in the dirt, the whole world became the site of my religion, and I could never isolate sacred ground because it was never different from any other ground. I couldn't find a particular holiness because holiness was all I saw if I bothered to look for it. And to this day I can't locate Zen for the same reason.

Pastor Rawlings touched me in a way that few ever have, and I love him for it and shame myself when I count his faith as merely simplistic. He knew the wisdom of falling to flat ground, and whatever doubts I have regarding his particular beliefs, such doubts pale in significance to the truth he once revealed to me in a dusty turkey yard years ago.

Oven-Breaker Monk

THERE ARE THINGS that need to be broken. Among these are unjust laws, for example, unwise policies once enacted that never served their intended purpose, promises made under pressure, attitudes and beliefs adopted when too young to choose otherwise, habits that have outlived their usefulness, old friendships clung to long after the affection that sustained them has waned, and perhaps even a worrisome old piece of china or some other knick-knack you've been protecting from breakage for years but considered too fragile and precious to put to use. This need for breakage is particularly apt for someone like myself who follows a religious or spiritual tradition. I can be particularly adept at making a spiritual project out of my life, with all sorts of ritual behaviors, attitudes, and beliefs set in place. It's when my enthusiasm for construction is at its highest that I most need to break up the whole elaborate and useless structure before it takes up all the room in my life.

An old Chinese story demonstrates this sort of spiritual demolition at work. The story goes that a monk, who's subsequently come to be known as the "Oven-Breaker Monk," lived in seclusion on Mount Sung. There he kept his solitary practice of meditation. Aside from this simple staple of all Zen followers, the Oven-Breaker Monk wasn't fond of other ritual enactments. He didn't maintain an altar in his small quarters, and he felt no need for incense, candles, and such. He did his daily zazen, kept a garden, gathered herbs when needed, and in general was content to care for the few obvious needs of his life. He wasn't a builder of spiritual structures of any sort, either of thought or of material. It's hard to imagine this old monk fussing, as I once did, over how many times to touch an incense stick to the forehead when making an offering at the altar or worrying over the proper sequence of bows and gong strikes during morning service.

It's told that one day, walking in a district that was home to some mountain aborigines, the Oven-Breaker Monk came upon a shrine that was sacred to the mountain's inhabitants. The shrine consisted of a hall that housed only an oven. The people of the mountain revered this oven and came from all about, unceasingly sacrificing to it by incinerating all sorts of living creatures. The Oven-Breaker Monk might very well have found the practice of burning up other creatures offensive, but the action that followed his discovery of the oven shrine seems directed less toward any moral objection and more toward the elaborate uselessness of the whole sacrificial ritual to which the mountain people lent themselves. Followed by a curious gathering of onlookers, the Oven-Breaker Monk went into the shrine and tapped once on the oven with his staff, and addressing this highly sacred oven, said, "What humbug! You're nothing more or less than brick and mud stuck together." Then he tapped it with his staff again, and the whole oven toppled over, broke, and collapsed into a heap on the shrine floor. In that instant, the mountain people witnessed their single, ancient religious practice reduced to a dusty pile before their very eyes.

Imagining that it was my sacred oven, now what do I do? It's pointless to cling to a belief that's been exposed as mere mud and bricks. But witnessing its apparent power to topple ovens, I might get curious about the staff the Oven-Breaker Monk carries. I might even be tempted to substitute a belief in the staff for my lost belief in the oven. But if I'm too quick to find something else to enshrine, nothing much will have changed.

What actually follows in the story gets quite interesting. With the stone lying in heaps, the spirit of the stove is released. And when the released spirit thanks the Oven-Breaker Monk for freeing him, the Oven-Breaker Monk declines to credit his own action and tells the spirit that it is his inherent nature that set him free. How many of those standing by that day realized that within the very mud and brick of life itself, there dwells a boundless and irrepressible nature? How many who toppled and broke apart rose empty and free from the dusty rubble.

I spend a fair amount of time breaking ovens. Zen is my religion, and I'm inclined to set up shrines in its behalf, some of them quite beautiful, constructed of the most principled and loving intent, deserving of devotion, thoroughly worthy of any sacrifice I might offer to them. But what I sacrifice to these conventional shrines of mine is invariably the untrammeled mind that would otherwise abide. Somehow what's asked of me is simpler than any ritual I can devise. One tap of the Oven-Breaker Monk's staff, and another structure of religious beauty crumbles and falls at my feet. I shovel out the mess and sweep up the dust, leaving the floor of the mind's temple free and clear of obstruction.

Property

THERE ARE LONG STRETCHES of the California coastline where you can't get to the beach without trespassing. The wave-washed rocks and strips of sandy beach lie beyond reach, somewhere behind the walls and gates of those whose money has bought themselves a view of the ocean for their own personal benefit. I don't see such behavior as driven so much by the wish to exclude others as by some curious lack of pleasure in things one doesn't own title to. It's like not being able to enjoy the presence of a beautiful woman or a marvelously expressive work of art or a picturesque landscape without your enjoyment being diminished by lack of possession.

Yet, while the *idea* of owning things is real enough to those who think in such terms, the actual owning of anything is questionable. We're all here for a finite duration, and as it's often said, "You can't take it with you." So the best one can claim for ownership is that it constitutes a term lease on the use of certain resources and properties. But since everyone in the world depends upon these same resources and properties, and since they were already here and in use when I arrived on the scene and will be used by others when I'm gone, it's folly to think that any of it is mine.

It might be a harmless enough folly to imagine that we actually own things if we didn't take our ownership rights so seriously and if we weren't so readily capable of destroying what we "own" in order to keep it. The possession of property rights is nearly synonymous with freedom and personal autonomy in the minds of most Americans, rich or impoverished. It's an unfortunate confusion that leads to the worst and most violent of our behaviors. People will kill each other over the ownership of things, mistakenly equating possession with freedom. The notion that I can do what I want with the things I own leads to the ambition to purchase individual freedom through acquisition, as if freedom were a commodity to be bought or stolen or fought for as the need might be.

Henry David Thoreau, who understood literally and intimately the self-canceling consequence of linking freedom with property, observed that wherever he happened to be at the moment the landscape radiated around him accordingly and that he already "owned" everything in sight as fully and completely as one holding legal title might. "Enjoy the land, but own it not. Through want of enterprise and faith men are where they are, buying and selling, and spending their lives like serfs." A freedom that relies on exercising control over territory has the diametrically opposed consequence of enslaving us to the very means we employ. We are left struggling to acquire through indirection what we already directly possess.

E. M. Forster, in his essay, "My Wood," tells of having bought a small property in the English countryside, and then proceeds to ask, "If you own things, what's their effect on you? What is the effect on me of my wood?" Among several psychological effects of owning a wood, one such effect is worth quoting here at length for its obvious relevance to the adverse relationship between freedom and territory:

> It makes me feel it ought to be larger. The other day I heard a twig snap in it. I was annoyed at first, for I thought that someone was blackberrying, and depreciating the value of the undergrowth. On coming nearer, I saw it was not a man who had trodden on the twig and snapped it, but a bird, and I felt pleased. My bird. The bird was not equally pleased. Ignoring the relation between us, it took flight as soon as it saw the shape of my face, and flew straight over the boundary hedge into a field, the property of Mrs. Henessy, where it sat down with a loud squawk. It had become Mrs. Henessy's bird. Something seemed grossly amiss here, something that would not have occurred had the wood been larger. I could not afford to buy Mrs. Henessy out, I dared not murder her, and limitations of this sort beset me on every side. . . . Nor was I comforted when Mrs. Henessy's bird took alarm for the second time and flew clean away from us all, under the belief that it belonged to itself.

In the end Forster sees no help for his predicament other than "I shall wall in and fence out until I really taste the sweets of property." And a bitter sweetness it is, having finally contrived to literally imprison himself within the confines of his purchase. Forster's ironic portrayal of the effect of land ownership on the human psyche is perfectly accurate as far as I can see. And he leaves us as an alternative the teasing image of the bird that can't be walled in or fenced out and, like everything else, belongs to itself.

KAREN AND I "OWN" A HOUSE on a quiet, tree-laden avenue in Chico, California. I sometimes find myself thinking of it as "ours." After all, we alone hold title to the property. It's fully paid for, and as long as I make timely payments on the property taxes, we won't be forced out into the street. But, then again, the house was first built in 1941 when I was only nine years old, and several families have bought and lived in it since that time—so the house I now live in had sheltered others for fifty-five years before I wrote a check to Mrs. Peterson for it and Karen and I moved in.

It occurs to me that this house of "ours" is actually a kind of communal house in which continuing occupancy has been sequential instead of simultaneous. I still feel the presence of those who've lived here before me and those who'll come after. I've discovered all sorts of odd little improvements prior owners have added to the property and from which I now benefit. And when I make repairs, re-roofing or painting the house, I sometimes feel as if I'm merely paying a debt to those who made repairs before me. I feel as if they and I are in this thing together, and the thing we're in is the maintenance of a house we all have a share in. And I hope the next owners will carry on with this obligation.

For the student of Zen, it's important to be skeptical of anything you regard as "yours." Everything from real estate to the living-room sofa to your toothbrush, right down to your very eyeballs and the air you breathe, is borrowed. Anything borrowed must be returned, and it is this attitude of return that informs the modesty and generosity of the Buddha Way.

I hold my entire life on loan in common with everyone else. If I can dispel from mind the vanity of possession and relax my grip on things, passing on whatever comes to hand, I will come in time to know things for themselves and not as belongings of any sort. Ownership is anathema to Zen not because ownership is evil as such, but because ownership is an intrinsically divisive delusion that inevitably leads to grasping and coveting.

To own something is to be owned by it. To free myself, I must let go.

The High Cost of Convenience

W E'RE A NATION that has opted for a standard of living based on the consumption of ease and convenience. And we're bored with it. Though we continue to opt for more and more convenience, deep down we really want to be a lot more alive than mere convenience allows for, often acting in ways that reveal an urgent longing to have something difficult and necessary in our lives. That's why problems are such fun and why trouble is fun and danger is fun, and why outrage and righteous indignation are sometimes the most fun of all. It's not that being wrought-up over something is the only way to feel alive or the best way or even a good way. Yet, almost any crisis can be terribly attractive to someone whose life consists mainly of avoiding effort and discomfort.

During the long years of the Cold War, when the stock market was steadily making gains and the gross national product grew annually and new technologies and labor-saving luxuries of all sorts were being bought up at an unprecedented rate, people staved off the sheer boredom of a life shorn of difficulty by keying on the threat of communist domination. As manufactured and patently false as the threat was, it could still be nursed for at least a modicum of excitement and even occasional feelings of energizing urgency.

Mikhail Gorbachev understood this perfectly when he told President Reagan, "I'm going to do something terrible to you. I'm going to deprive you of an enemy." Gorbachev no doubt realized that Reagan's demonizing of the Soviet Union as "the evil empire" was a tool for rallying citizen support for his policies and that the sudden refusal of the Soviet Union to accommodate itself to the role of an enemy would deprive Western leaders of an effective means of citizen control. But he no doubt understood as well the psychology of the citizens themselves for whom the Communist threat served to dispel some of the tedium of a life gone too soft.

A foot rub lacks pleasure if you haven't walked far enough to get sore feet. A hot shower is a bland event if you haven't gotten dirty. Rest is pointless if you're not tired. A meal is a matter of indifference to one who's not hungry. Nothing in life is genuinely pleasurable if it hasn't been purchased by some degree of direct effort. The human spirit languishes when it is not answerable to immediate and present necessity. If our most basic needs are provided without asking more of us than that we present an unexpired credit card, we tend to go credit-card-crazy, trying to extract from its frequent use some convincing semblance of providing for ourselves. We begin to measure accomplishment more by what we're able to purchase than by what we can actually do for ourselves. But there are only so many things one can buy that are really needed, and after those few necessities are satisfied, one's left with the boredom of purchasing endless conveniences.

Yet cravings for ease and convenience, cultivated in the psychological tactics of consumer advertising, render whole nations

addicted to their relentless pursuit. Students of Buddhism will recognize here the plight of the hungry ghost, the Buddhist metaphor
for those with an insatiable appetite. The hungry ghost can never
satisfy itself because its very nature is one of craving, and no amount
of acquisition will put that nature to rest.

Yet not everyone falls victim to the prospect of having things go
easy. I think of the old Zen master who, having grown old and
somewhat feeble, still insisted on doing his share of scrubbing and
mopping and sweeping and weeding the monastery garden. His
students, in pity for his old age, hid his tools from him. But
deprived of work, the master refused to eat. A life without necessary effort wasn't worth his sustaining. I understand his persuasion perfectly. Personally I think comfort is overrated. The day that
convenience takes the last tool from my own hands and turns the
work I've always done for myself over to the manufacturers of mass
production, leaving me idle and dependent, the necessity of my
labors will be forfeited, and I'll be left with little worth doing. And
were I bedridden as I have been at times and certainly will be
again, I would hope that I would willingly take on the long labor of
sickness and do the necessary work of illness for myself without
forfeiting the task to medical specialists or seeking its avoidance
altogether in some comforting state of prescribed sedation. The
human physical organism is a composite of earthly elements.
We're the offspring of sunlight, water, air, and of broken rock carried down the mountain slopes to rot into soil. We've been seed
and leaf and grass. We've swum the seas and crawled onto the continents. We've sprouted wings and taken to the skies. We've
climbed into the trees, grazed upon fields of grass, dug for roots,
tilled the soil, and planted corn and potatoes. We are creatures of
the earth, delivered of the earth, sustained by the earth. Our bodies
are made wholly of the earth's own substance. When we weaken the

intimacy of this bond in favor of machine-cultured convenience and ease, we suffer the loss of our natural selves.

IN MY TOWN OF CHICO, CALIFORNIA, there are only a small fraction of us who still rake leaves by hand. Hand raking is a task where one falls into the rhythm of it, stroking away at the ground with smooth sweeping movements, the drag of the rake, the musty smell of the leaves, the bending, lifting, and stacking of great armfuls of sycamore, pistachio, oak, dogwood, and maple leaves into piles at the curbside for the city crew to pick up. Those of us who do this are a bit of an historic oddity. If I were to modernize and succumb to the lure of a leaf blower, all I'd have to do is grab for the leaf blower, pour in some gas, yank the motor into action, and hit the yard with the engine strapped to my back and ear plugs stuffed in my ears to muffle the high-pitched whine of the thing. But my only connection with the leaves themselves, as with my body, would be effectively reduced to squeezing the trigger and directing the spout in the right direction. The only advantage over raking is that I could get the job done without having to bother with it very long.

The same is true of mowing the lawn with a simple, manual lawnmower. With a gasoline mower I wouldn't feel the resistance of the grass or hear the little click of the cutting blades as the mower is pushed over the lawn. I wouldn't hear the children laughing next door either or the birds squabbling over the dogwood berries or the chirp of a squirrel in the pistachio tree. I wouldn't smell the fresh cut grass very well either, which I'd have traded in for the smell of gasoline fumes and exhaust.

Our kitchens are equally motorized for convenience with mixers and food processors of all sorts, electric can openers, knife sharpeners, dishwashers, bread makers, frozen TV dinners, and microwave ovens. Who sharpens a knife on a simple stone these days? Who chops vegetables by hand? Who peels and cores an apple with a paring knife? I often thicken whipped cream with a hand mixer when I have friends in for dinner, and they line up to give it a try. It's become that much of a novelty. With so much of the cutting, stirring, mixing, blending, kneading, washing, and drying given over to machines, we've cancelled the body's intimate connection with the very food that gives us life. With all the labors that can be easily dispatched by machinery, we end up taking memberships at the local fitness club and substitute thirty minutes on a treadmill for a walk in the park.

You MIGHT THINK THAT ZEN encourages a low standard of living but in fact Zen encourages no standard of living at all. The mind of Zen is not a mind that differentiates between difficult and easy. My intent is not one of disparaging all comfort. A student of Zen is perfectly happy to take a nap, but doesn't perceive ease as inherently preferable to effort. At monasteries and Zen centers where I have trained, we invariably undertake periods of working meditation. Most of the work consists of simple manual labors—chopping vegetables, cooking, washing and drying the plates and pots and utensils we use, sweeping floors and raking the walkways, taking out the garbage, and cleaning the restrooms.

I like the practice of work meditation. The work itself, and the working together as a team, and the fact that the work isn't mere make-work, but work necessary to the real running of things, serves to awaken the body to its own natural state, drawing us intimately into the body of life itself. I've tilled the soil with teams of horses and know what it is to follow on foot the rainbow sheen of fresh cut earth. I've breathed the rank sweetness of upturned soil, felt the strain and creak of harness telegraphed to me along the length of the reins. And I've ridden tractors as well, crisscrossing the field on rolling wheels, the throb of the engine in my ears, the smell of gasoline exhaust in my nostrils, where I sit suspended above the earth, the intimate connection and step-by-step knowledge of the land forfeited to convenience and speed. It's not good enough to settle for such false comfort, for it will fail us. I know the loss firsthand, and it's greater than any of us imagines. We need the tug of the harness, we need the pull and the strain of cutting our way through the fields of our lives.

I saw a woman once who'd undertaken to sand and refinish an old weathered hardwood table that sat in the shade of a black oak tree outside the monastery guest quarters. She worked on it every spare moment she had, and over the period of a ten-day retreat, the table grew smoother and smoother until you could actually catch a faint reflection of yourself in its surface if the light was just right. I'd see her there during rest periods up on the tabletop on her knees sanding and polishing away. She'd gone from a coarser 80-grit sandpaper to 100-grit to a nearly smooth 120. At times she merely rubbed the surface with a rag of cloth. When I inquired, she told me that she'd never done any work like that before. "I've never really done a job," she said. When the retreat was over and the others were leaving, she was still at the task, putting the finishing touches to the table while there was still enough evening light to work by.

The Poor Thing

THE BUDDHA WAY is characterized by generosity, a quality that results in the willingness to accept what life gives without complaint. In Robert Louis Stevenson's *The Poor Thing* this modest acceptance is truthfully portrayed:

There was a man in the islands who fished for his bare bellyful, and took his life in his hands to go forth upon the sea between four planks. But though he had much ado, he was merry of heart; and the gulls heard him laugh when the spray met him. And though he had little lore, he was sound of spirit; and when the fish came to his hook in the mid-waters, he blessed God without weighing. He was bitter poor in goods and bitter ugly of countenance, and he had no wife.

With so little of material goods or fortunate circumstance, the Poor Thing is nonetheless joyous of spirit and thankful for whatever is given him. Later when the Poor Thing came into possession of a single rusty horseshoe, he was told by another that, "It is a thing of no price for it is rusty." But the Poor Thing replied, "In my thought one thing is as good as another in this world; and a shoe of a horse will do." In seeing that one thing is as good as another, the Poor Thing has touched upon the very heart of Zen. What he *has* will do. What he *is* will do. He asks for no improvement in his situation or in himself. By comparison, I am shamed by my own quibbling dissatisfactions with life, my arguments with what circumstance has brought me. The attitude of making do with what I have and what I am is the attitude of every genuinely free person in the long history of the human species.

WHEN MY BROTHER, ROWLAND, and I were small boys living on a leased farm in Southern California's Orange County, the nation was in the midst of World War II. Our family was quite poor in those days, as were other farm families in the county. Most families could feed themselves from their own gardens but had little cash, and it took the work of a whole family to keep a farm going. What purchases a family could afford were further limited by rationing. But on Saturdays, if Rowland and I got our chores done on time, we were given a quarter each for the matinee at the Gem Theatre in Garden Grove. We'd walk the five miles to town where we hooked up with the town kids to watch the double feature that the Gem Theater always ran. The movies were invariably of three kinds: cowboy movies, gangster movies, or war movies. I don't know to this day if any of our parents knew what scenes of violence and mayhem we kids were being subjected to.

Toy cap pistols were popular in those days, and several of the boys would come to the matinee armed with holsters and cap guns belted round their waists. And after the movie, we'd gather in a vacant lot adjacent to the feed store and play cops and robbers, cowboys and Indians, or fight World War II. We dodged about behind stacked pallets, parked delivery trucks, or mounds of baled hay. The boys with cap pistols could jump out at you and squeeze down on the trigger, and the hammer of the pistol would slap closed on a cap and a little explosion would sound. But Rowland and I had to make do with a pointed finger and a thumb cocked up, settling for whatever shooting sounds we could make with our mouths. We both wanted cap pistols of our own, and when birthdays or Christmases came round, that's what we asked for. But in those days our gifts were necessarily practical, like jeans or shirts or school shoes. Yet, one Christmas, along with a little package of clothing, we each got a small pocketknife as well. I remember being disappointed that the knives weren't pistols and put mine away in a drawer in case I found some use for it. But Rowland's knife went into his pocket, where he could reach in and feel it there if he wanted to.

He whittled on soft wood first, shaping surprisingly realistic versions of cows and pigs and even a little cup with a handle you could actually drink from. And then, he began to seek out harder woods, which while more difficult to whittle, produced sounder results. He'd sit on the edge of a shed roof by the garden patch and whittle away for hours with little shavings of wood falling to ground below. Then one day, Rowland set to work on a three-and-a-half foot length of maple with a width and thickness of about two inches by four inches. The carving was slow going, but by degrees the unmistakable stock of a rifle appeared, and then a trigger guard and trigger, and a rear sight, and gradually a perfectly round barrel with a forward sight mounted on its tip, and the end of the barrel hollowed out so that at a glance it appeared as if the barrel was hollow for its entire length. It was a thing of astounding realism, carved out of a single uninterrupted length of maple by a boy of nine years who'd discovered that if life hadn't given him the cap pistol he wanted, then a pocket knife to carve out a gun of his own making would do just as well. On Saturdays where we boys shot up the countryside and each other in the vacant lot after matinees, Rowland was offered all sort of trades for the coveted rifle, the best being that of a pair of matching cap pistols with holsters and a gun belt, but Rowland was content to keep what he had.

SOMETHING RATHER MARVELOUS occurs when we decide that what we have and what we are will do. Prior sources of complaint convert to occasions for gratitude and praise. Instead of finding ourselves lacking in something, whatever we are and whatever comes to us is received as a gift. Karen, out walking in the park two days ago as I write this, saw the late autumn leaves falling through the chill morning air from above—broad sycamore leaves drifting lazily downward and compact little oak leaves falling swiftly. She thought to catch one of them, and when a little nine-lobed valley oak leaf came to rest in her upturned palm, she blessed earth and sky and tree without weighing.

The Meek

THERE'S A RIGHTEOUS SORT OF YIELDING, much akin to the unassuming modesty of Zen, to be found in the Eight Beatitudes of Jesus's Sermon on the Mount, particularly when he declares, "Blessed are the meek for they shall inherit the earth." An inheritance typically takes place when a generation or individual has passed away and handed down something to the heirs. Who in Jesus's declaration has passed away? Who are these meek who have inherited the earth and what sort of earth has been handed them? *Meek* entered English during the Middle English period, a word of Scandinavian origin akin to the Old Norse *mjukr* meaning "soft" and "gentle." If the meek are soft and gentle, then perhaps what has passed away in their lives is the world of the hard and rough and what they've subsequently inherited is the world of the soft and gentle. The meek are the ones who show patience and accept their lot without complaint. They are the ones who endure insult and even injury without nursing resentment. The meek are without pretension, the ones Zen Master Lin-chi describes as "persons of no rank whose faces go in and out the gates of humankind."

In *Shambhala: The Sacred Path of the Warrior*, Chögyam Trungpa refers to meekness as a dignity devoid of arrogance. "Meek," he writes, "does not mean being feeble; it just means resting in a state of simplicity, being uncomplicated and, at the same time, approachable. Whether others are hostile or friendly, the warrior of the meek extends a sense of kindness to himself and mercy to others." It's through this unforced and uncalculated modesty that the warrior of the meek inherits the earth. The earth is home to those who don't put themselves at odds with it, who keep house respectfully and without an undue show of ambition.

Of course there are those who make a public display out of humility—the kind that can out-humble any competitor and is damn proud of it. In *Great Expectations*, Charles Dickens dubbed one such character "the bully of humility." The meek I have in mind make no claim to virtuous behavior at all. They simply do what comes to hand because it appears to need doing. They think no more or less of themselves regardless of whether they manage to succeed in effecting a good result as a consequence of their efforts or fail to effect any noticeable result at all. I don't count myself among these meek as I describe them here. I'm too willful in temperament to make the grade, though I suppose my admittance to this failing is a semblance of humility after all.

But I've known some who *have* made the grade, and among these is Hector Berrens, whom my father hired to work on the farm along with Hector's retarded brother, Ernie, who could only work effectively under Hector's personal supervision. Hector, a squat, muscled man, with powerful shoulders, arms, and legs, had emigrated from Belgium. He bore a broad forehead, unflinching eyes, and thick dark hair. When he stood he always seemed solidly rooted and when he worked he was the human equivalent of a draft horse. But as unlikely as his appearance might suggest, Hector was as gentle and sweet and kind as anyone I've ever known. I was a boy when I was first introduced to Hector, and he took my small hand into his broad calloused paw and shook hands with me as gently as he might hold a chick newly hatched from the farm incubator. I felt the firmness of him then but nothing of strain or forced effort. I was to learn in time that Hector was a man completely at home in his own skin, content to be as he was without intending to be any way at all. He was utterly innocent of self-appraisal.

On the job, Hector took care of himself and Ernie without a thought of contending with others for advantage or advancement of any sort. He accepted the hardest and dirtiest work without objection and with no apparent concern regarding who was being spared the dirty work through his effort. But he'd accept the easiest work as well on the few occasions it was offered him. At noon in the lunchroom, debates sometimes arose among the other field-hands. They'd argue the relative merits of the Republican Party versus the Democrats, Fords versus Chevrolets, and Catholics versus Protestants (though there wasn't a Catholic among them). On one occasion, they got into a rather heated debate over whether Morris, as they called my father in my presence, should agree to a profit-sharing plan like the one in the sugar beet refinery a few miles down the road. They thought it only fair, since they did all the hard work. They didn't worry that I'd expose them to my father because I was contentious in those days and fancied myself a rebel in the cause of the underdog. Since my father was boss, all the rest of us were underdogs by my simple calculation. The men knew this and often enlisted my support for their complaints. Hector never entered into these debates, but on the day of the profit-sharing argument, with feelings running high, one of the men asked, "What do you think, Hector?" "Ernie and I make enough to feed ourselves, pay rent, and take care of our parents," Hector said. "If I need more, I'll ask Morris for it." Hector didn't dodge controversy, he just wasn't reactive to it. He had the humility to not require of himself an opinion to be heard.

Ernie was a slight little man. He trotted along behind Hector wherever he went, looking nervously about and advancing in little stops and starts like a squirrel crossing the street. He did whatever Hector told him to. Once in a while though, he'd suddenly fly into a rage, shouting at Hector over some imagined wrong, his body shaking, his face suddenly red, snot running from his nose. Hector would wait him out for a minute or two, and then he'd go to him and put an arm around him until he calmed down. He'd wipe his nose with a handkerchief, and they'd both go back to work. When their old Belgian father died and their mother had taken to bed determined to follow her husband into the grave, Ernie was inconsolable. He'd be following along behind Hector when grief would suddenly overwhelm him and he'd stop right there in the midst of the work, standing in the field, shaking and crying with grief. When Hector would realize Ernie was no longer with him, he'd go back to get him, and once I saw Hector take Ernie up in his arms and rock him back and forth and sing something to him that sounded to me like a lullaby from Belgium.

SURELY HECTOR BERRENS WAS Chögyam Trungpa's warrior of the meek, bearing a dignity devoid of arrogance, uncomplicated and approachable, extending a sense of kindness to himself and others. He could be this way because he didn't rely on the willful exercise of force to shape a world to his own ends. He didn't require admiration or insist on having things his way, and so had little need to assert or defend himself. He could afford to be soft and gentle—one of the blessed meek whom Jesus said inherits the earth.

Public Ethics

W HEN I RECOGNIZE the ground you stand on as being the very same ground I stand on, I move beyond a purely private ethic to a public ethic. In realizing our moral and situational proximity, I become responsible for you as much as for myself. What I choose to do no longer concerns me alone but involves you as well. The surface of my skin is no longer the outermost limit of who I am, a boundary to be protected against intrusion, but rather a permeable medium of exchange between myself and others. When I am opened up in this way, I no longer know where I begin and where I end. Political, cultural, and social boundaries become artificial and arbitrary. It's a very public thing in which, divested of any purely private self, I travel disembodied, or, perhaps more accurately, variously embodied, among the endless alternate lives I might well be living if I weren't living the one I'm currently in.

I engaged one such alternate life yesterday when I came upon a homeless vagrant outside the downtown post office. He was a man in his fifties or early sixties. His clothes were soiled with a sort of sooty looking grime. He wore an incongruous floral Hawaiian shirt, missing buttons and frayed at the cuffs, and a pair of pants stiffened with dirt and sweat that were too big for him and were held up by a length of rope tied at the waist. He wanted money. I said, "Sorry," and was about to move on when I saw in his eyes a weariness and defeat that I'd once seen reflected in my own eyes looking back at me from the mirrors of an earlier time. "I only need three more dollars for a pack of cigarettes," he explained. "I know where I can get them cheap. I've got almost enough. Three bucks more will do it." "I don't want to encourage you to smoke," I said. "Look," he said, "I'm dry ten days now. Not a drop. I can't quit cigarettes and booze at the same time." I remembered then when I wanted a drink so badly that I would have done anything to distract myself from the craving. "You're right," I said. "You can't do both at once," and I gave him the money he'd asked for.

PUBLIC ETHICS CAN'T BE PRIVATIZED because we can't really extricate our private affairs from the affairs of others. Psychologists refer to "enmeshment" as an unfortunate incapacity to distinguish one's self from others, a sort of emotional entrapment in which the enmeshed individual can't or won't act on her own—but this is not the circumstance to which I'm referring. Private ethics are public ethics precisely because we *can* act on our own, and because our actions, no matter how private and individual they may seem, invariably affect others. At times we can see this clearly. I lose my temper and scold a child and the child cries or his eyes go cold or he shouts back at me or flips me the finger. But we often cannot discern the effect we're having on others. What are the consequences of what I say or don't say at the family breakfast table, whether I acknowledge others or show them the backside of the daily newspaper? What's the consequence of rinsing off my own dishes and stacking them to dry rather than leaving a bowl crusted with oatmeal for someone else to clean up? What's the consequence of letting someone merge into freeway traffic without insisting on my right-of-way? And what effect does the mood I carry to my work or to the gas station or the supermarket have on those I make contact with?

The fact that I can't possibly trace the myriad possible consequences of my actions doesn't absolve me from responsibility for my relationship to these consequences. I've had a teacher who was quick to point out to me that it's not my business what others think of me or choose to do in regard to my behavior. This is sound enough advice against neurotic enmeshment or meddling in other's lives or trying to fix the world in general. But I don't think the teacher meant I wasn't responsible for the way I dealt with others. I think he would say that doing the best I can in regard to others is my business. But he would add the caveat that once I've done the best I know to do, the rest is someone else's business. This is the public ethic I would prescribe to myself as well. I would tell myself to be conscious of the reciprocal and radiating consequences of human interchange and to do the best I can to affect others in kindly and considerate ways, but to not presume to manage the lives of others.

Zen is often thought of as an internalized religious practice involved in acquiring personal enlightenment. But those of us who undertake the path of Zen come in time to know that there is no separate person to be so enlightened. Either we wake up together or none of us awakens at all. It is this recognition of a common, inseparable humanity that constitutes enlightenment and it is the failure of this recognition that dooms us to lives of mutual antagonism and distrust. Every private hope I might cling to, every private fear or aversion, is in truth a public matter that can't be privately resolved. It is so, because what I am and what I do can't be disentangled from the mutual and reciprocal influence of others. The care I take of my private life is undertaken as a public obligation. The needs of others are my needs as well.

Refuge

A TIBETAN SCHOLAR once complained to me of Zen's severe reductionism. The scholar was right: Zen is so reductive by nature that it actually self-destructs! The longer I practice Zen the less I have of anything, including Zen itself. When Zen gets done with its work, what's left? In part, what's left is the one place of genuine refuge. There's a sense in which all the classical koan stories of the Zen tradition invite the student to discover this place of refuge.

In the ninety-sixth case of the *Blue Cliff Record*, Zen Master Chao-chou instructs his followers with the following three "turning words": "A gold Buddha does not pass through a furnace; a wood Buddha does not pass through fire; a mud Buddha does not pass through water." And then he adds, "The real Buddha sits within." Yuan-wu in his commentary to this koan points out that "If a mud Buddha passes through water it will dissolve; if a gold Buddha passes through a furnace it will melt; if a wood Buddha passes through fire it will burn up."

I can't speak for anyone else, but the circumstance Chao-chou describes seems perfectly consonant with the particulars of my own life. I can vouch for life's various meltings, burnings, and dissolvings, as well as the fact that nothing with a fixed name such as "Buddha" or "Lin Jensen" ever gets through life with its identity intact. What does get through is stripped of individuated being. You don't get into the refuge bearing merely personal distinction.

Chao-chou might seem to have set up a dichotomy between the "real Buddha" whom he says "sits within" and the "imitation" Buddha made of gold, wood, and mud, until one asks what it is that the real Buddha sits within? Where is the true Buddha's house? The second Zen ancestor, Hui-k'o, was on such a quest when he pleaded with Bodhidharma to set his troubled mind at rest and Bodhidharma said he would do so if Hui-k'o would only bring him his mind. But, having exhausted all possible means of locating his mind, Hui-k'o had to own that he could find no such thing. Hui-k'o's mind had proved to be indistinguishable from anything else he encountered in his search. The rice farmer with the ox, the ox itself, the paddy with the rice shoots appearing, the bowl of fruit at an inn, the dust rising from the path, all were nothing but his mind. Hui-k'o's mind, as it turned out, was not something to be found *nowhere* in particular but rather *everywhere* in particular. With no separate mind to be found, Bodhidharma had put Hui-k'o's mind to rest. In the same way, the real Buddha is not separate from gold, wood, and mud. The real Buddha lives in the house of fire, water, and furnace, and the true refuge is exactly that dissolving and melting and burning that characterizes our ordinary lives. By whatever metaphor portrayed, it's the dissolution of self that brings one to refuge.

I've tried and, like Hui-k'o, I couldn't find my mind either, which is more or less like losing sight of myself. It's as if I were run through Chao-chou's furnace where all the individuated identities are reduced to ash. With no familiar or clearly discernible mind, it's impossible to know who I am, because whoever I thought I was turns out not to be me at all. That moment of self-vacancy, of not knowing who I am, is, for all its fleeting uncertainties, the very threshold of the Buddha Refuge. And the reason this refuge is initially frightening is that it can't be sorted out or understood or identified in any of the mind's familiar ways. Refuge comes without a tag attached. It resists being anything in particular and seems to float among endlessly shifting possibilities. It can't be fixed in place by thought and won't hold still the way an *idea* of myself can be fixed and held still. Refuge is always melting down or burning itself up or dissolving like sugar in water.

I GREW UP ON A FARM, and I can't remember a time in my youth when I didn't dream of having a farm of my own. By the time I was nine, I subscribed to the *Western Livestock Journal*, which I read every month from cover to cover. I sent off for government pamphlets on raising poultry and on the cultivation of row crops. I couldn't imagine a life for myself other than that of farming. In time, I realized that I couldn't expect to remain on the home farm, because it was understood that the home farm, where my older brother, Rowland, had taken over management, couldn't support another family. But when I was drafted into the army and about to be shipped overseas, my father let me know that when my tour of duty was over, he'd put me to managing and farming some acreage he'd acquired at the southern tip of the Salton Sea in Southern California's Imperial Valley. The Imperial Valley farm was perfect for row crops, particularly winter vegetables there where the lake water warmed the air enough to prevent freezing. So this was the answer to my being a working partner in the family and the farmer I'd always wanted to be.

Despite all the new things there were to see and understand during the two years I served in Germany, the anticipation of coming back to a farm of my own was seldom out of mind. I sent to the Department of Agriculture for more government pamphlets on various aspects of row-crop farming. I designed schedules of planting, watering, and harvesting geared to the Imperial Valley seasons. I even drew diagrams of crop rotations scaled to the size and configuration of the actual property. It's curious though that of all the letters that passed between my parents and me, I don't recall ever writing to them of these activities and anticipations. For one thing, Father seldom wrote at all and Mother was more interested in what life was like for me in a foreign country.

So when I was discharged and got back home, I didn't think much of it at first when Father didn't say anything about the Imperial Valley farm. But within a week, in a casual comment to my brother at the lunch table, Father made mention of the sale of the property a year and a half before. It had been sold within the first six months of my overseas tour of duty. Father hadn't said anything about that fact on my return because he hadn't even remembered his plans to put me to work there. I never bothered to remind him.

But afterward, I felt as if I'd been plucked out of the only life I'd ever fancied for myself, like a boat cut loose from its mooring, drifting on a strangely indifferent sea. And all the options were quickly shut down by the takeover of corporate farming, which made it virtually impossible to start a family farm from scratch the way my father once had. For all practical purposes the dream of a lifetime had been cancelled once and for all, and the "person" of the boy and youth who dreamt those dreams was gone as well. Now that I was not the boy with a farm in his future, I simply didn't know who I was.

There have been other times of the sort with which most humans can relate: the time a teenage girlfriend broke up with me and I thought I couldn't live without her, or the time an industrial accident at Anderson Plywood mill in Northern California left me so stunned that I lost all memory of events until after some yet unknown passage of time I found myself working in an Orange County paint plant 400 miles to the south, not knowing how I got there. And then there was the time when, after 24 years of marriage, I was asked to move out and found myself in a rented room at the rear of some stranger's house, shocked to realize that while it's possible to fall in love, it's possible to fall out of love as well. These were times when the last comfortingly familiar thought of "me" was lost to chance's shifting circumstance, the interim time between "persons" with the old person gone and no substitute yet in sight. Still, even when the last vestige of a "self" has melted, burned, or dissolved, there's still something left. And if I can make acquaintance with what's left, I will have taken refuge in the Buddha's household.

ONE CAN DRAW A TENUOUS SECURITY from knowing who and what one is, residing in an identity like "farmer" as I once did, or "teacher" as I eventually did, or "husband," "parent," and so forth. But such a self is not a secure refuge, because it's conditional, reliant on circumstances, imposed and sustained by thought. You can hunt for such a self, but all you'll ever uncover is the shape and shadow of your own thoughts. When the thoughts I have of me are no longer convincing, I'll have come at last to rest on the solid bedrock beneath the shifting soils of chance.

The Three Defilements

THERE ARE THREE SO-CALLED DEFILEMENTS in Buddhist psychology that are typically translated into English as greed, aversion, and delusion. These three defilements are derived from the Buddha's formulation of the Four Noble Truths. In accord with the Buddha's teaching and the evidence of my own experience, they comprise the source of most human suffering. Greed drives us to cling to or hoard the things we want, and aversion drives us to avoid and resist what we don't want. Delusion is the folly of thinking we can get what we want to the exclusion of what we don't want. It's an attempt to split up circumstances into categories of our own devising. But reality is not divisible in that way, and the irony of such a delusion resides in a failure to recognize that greed and aversion are psychologically one and the same. My clinging to something I want is always in resistance to something I don't want. My resistance to something I don't want resides in my preference for something I do want.

It's a situation that leaves me pushing away and pulling in simultaneously, a matter of considerable strain. When I put myself at odds with circumstance, I am certain to suffer just as the Buddha said I would. The competition of contraries engaged in between clinging and aversion nullifies the effective force of either, and the resultant stalemate effectively shuts down the capacity for healthy human exchange, confining me within my own likes and dislikes.

Greed and aversion aren't necessarily all-or-nothing states, both occurring in varying degrees and kinds. Jealousy and envy are instructive in this regard, ranging from states of minor discomfort to those of consuming passions. Not only that, but these particular forms of coveting demonstrate the invariable simultaneity of attraction and aversion. If I'm held in the throes of jealousy, that's because I want to possess a particular object or person to the exclusion of others. I'm left suspended between the will to include and exclude, a state that's emotionally self-canceling since I obviously can't do both. It's a matter of reeling in and tossing out at the same time.

But jealousy and envy also point unmistakably to the source of this simultaneity, which is seen to reside in threatened identity, a protective defense on behalf of the idea one holds of one's "self." If, as in jealousy, I'm distressed by the attention someone gives to someone other than me, it's because I somehow feel diminished by that loss. The critical possessiveness that drives me into jealousy is not found so much in the desire to possess the coveted object itself as in the manner in which the object of possession reflects on me. Which means that what I'm actually trying to protect is my *idea* of myself, which leaves me straining to maintain possession of the conditions necessary to support the "person" I think I am. If I'm coveting your house, job, wife, car, success, or fame that's because I feel less of a person with them in your possession than in mine. If

I can't match or exceed your acquisitions and successes, I'm drawn into doubt regarding myself. I need what you have in order to be the person I want to be.

However, if I'm attracted to something *for its own sake* and don't feel personally diminished by its absence, then that's quite another thing. The same is true of aversion. I may not like rudeness in a person, but if I'm not favorably comparing myself to the rude person, then the aversion is not necessarily rooted in identity. It's possible to check this out. Suppose I'm running for a seat on the city council and my opponent wins the seat; I may very well be disappointed because after all I lost and I'm only human. But it's equally a human response for me to be glad for my opponent's success, understanding that he wanted to win as much as I. Supposing I win the seat, I may be very pleased and happy with my success. I wanted to win, didn't I? But in my pleasure, am I also capable of sympathizing with the loser's disappointment? If I can find the degree of graciousness within me that allows me to exchange myself with others, then my simple likes and dislikes, for whatever difficulties they might possibly bring me, are not rooted in identity. However both the poor loser and the poor winner struggle between fancied esteem and disesteem that ultimately drives the forces of greed, aversion, and delusion. Such a qualified identity is a casualty of conflicting preference, a "self" strung out between poles of attraction and aversion.

Indulging greed and aversion shrinks the world down to the exact dimensions of my own likes and dislikes. Every fixed opinion, judgment, and belief of mine serves to further isolate me within walls constructed of anger, jealousy, envy, distrust, and, most of all, fear. My whole reality becomes a threatening standoff between what is perceived as inside and what is outside, with me huddled on the inside behind the barriers fear constructs, clutching my little treasure of preferences and apprehensive over possible interference from without. When I give in to greed and aversion, I have taken residence in the house of delusion.

The three defilements are actually gifts given us if we receive them as such, because they point the way out of the suffering that each brings. But they will only do so if we acknowledge them and their presence in our lives. It's when I admit my greed for getting what I want and my aversion toward what I don't want, that I am able to see through these pointless and competing preferences. If I can just once pry open the tight fist of greed, the hand of generosity is revealed. I needn't *try* to be generous; I only have to let go of what I'm hanging on to. The relinquishing is itself the generosity. The same is true of aversion. What I don't push away will enter of its own accord and will no longer seem so foreign and threatening to me, opening a pathway to acceptance, and even love, for what was once feared and avoided.

Of course I can always incarcerate myself behind walls of greed, aversion, and delusion. Yet even the slightest curiosity reveals that the walls of my friendless cell are merely constructed of my own self-concern and troubled apprehensions.

Just beyond the furthest point of fear hang the keys to turn the lock that sets me free.

Fair and Foul

CRAZY JANE TALKS TO THE BISHOP

I met the Bishop on the road
And much said he and I.
"Those breasts are flat and fallen now,
Those veins must soon be dry;
Live in a heavenly mansion,
Not in some foul sty."

"Fair and foul are near of kin,
And fair needs foul," I cried.
"My friends are gone, but that's a truth
Nor grave nor bed denied,
Learned in bodily lowliness
And in the heart's pride.

"A woman can be proud and stiff
When on love intent;
But Love has pitched his mansion in
The place of excrement;
For nothing can be sole or whole
That has not been rent."
—WILLIAM BUTLER YEATS

Contemporary lay Zen students are frequently troubled by all sorts of thoughts and behaviors that they perceive as standing in the way of their spiritual progress. They complain of being given to bouts of anger, fear, doubt, or error. What students invariably want to do with these traits is get rid of them. In their quest for improvement, it rarely occurs to them to rid themselves of their self-dissatisfaction. They're convinced that they're not okay, and won't be until they rid themselves of their faults.

One young woman came to dokusan complaining of how "wimpy" she was. "I lack courage," she said. "I'm afraid of my own shadow." When I suggested that perhaps she wasn't fearful enough, she replied that she could hardly rid herself of fear by indulging it. "You've tried to get rid of it," I pointed out, "and it hasn't worked. If it keeps hanging around, it might have something to tell you. It might want to be your friend." She left the session with my encouragement to invite fear into her life. As she did so, she came to realize that she wasn't such a "fraidy cat" after all. "When I got acquainted with it, fear taught me a lot," she told me. "I discovered that most of my fears weren't that scary once I quit resisting them, and some of my fears were warranted, like not walking alone through the student section after dark on a party night." She sat across from me grinning and pleased with herself. What she said next revealed the depth of her recent insight. "I wanted courage," she said, "and I found out that there is no courage without fear. You don't get one without the other."

Students are typically disappointed when I counsel appreciation of their "faults." But in doing so, I follow a central teaching of Zen, the classical expression of which is attributed to an exchange between a Chinese Zen master, Chao-chou, and a monk whose concern was like that of my own students. Chao-chou told his congregation that Buddha causes passion in all of us. When a monk asked, "How do we get rid of it?" Chao-chou replied with a provocative question of his own: "Why should we get rid of it?"

Chao-chou reminds us that we never get anywhere by trying to leave ourselves behind. His response suggests that we might do well to consider what we're throwing away.

CRAZY JANE SAID IT BEST OF ALL. In William Butler Yeats's *Crazy Jane Talks to the Bishop*, the Bishop takes the ragged, aged Crazy Jane to task for the life she's lived. The Bishop's system of ethics draws a sharp distinction between spirit and body, holy and profane, pure and impure. His view of the world is like old parchment, sucked dry of anything that's lively, disordered, or subject to chance. He dismisses Crazy Jane's life of unrestrained sensuality as foul and unworthy. Because he seeks to avoid life itself, he has no better defense against the intrusion of life than to trot out the usual righteous cant about the sins of earthly indulgence, accusing Crazy Jane of having lived in a foul sty and urging her to opt for a heavenly mansion before it's too late.

Crazy Jane owns up to his accusation, but insists that fair and foul are in fact inseparable, complimentary qualities of life. For Crazy Jane, life's a matter of risking the heart, and the Bishop's prudish discretion is utterly foreign to her. She's in this world for love, and is unimpressed by the Bishop's antiseptic injunctions against the heart's affections. She counters the Bishop's call to live in a heavenly mansion with the reminder that "Love has pitched his mansion in the place of excrement." For Crazy Jane, love is not selective, but inclusive and whole. Speaking from the wounds of a life fully spent, she tells the Bishop, "Nothing can be sole or whole that has not been rent."

Yet for all his ethical rigidity, the Bishop's point is one that lies at the heart of the Buddha's teaching of the Four Noble Truths: namely, that clinging to sensory desires is a source of self-imposed suffering. Most who have set foot on the Buddhist path will recognize from personal experience the ways in which unchecked passions can lead to harm and suffering. I can't argue with the Bishop that such greedy indulgence is unworthy and a source of eventual disappointment and suffering. We do well to exercise reasonable caution, knowing when to say "no" to the very thing we most want. There's a touching and inherent modesty in putting one's desires aside for the sake of mutual harmony and the common good. The Bishop's mistake is in assuming that Crazy Jane is wrongfully clinging to worldly desires while he is not. He's wrong on both counts.

The Bishop has split his world into a simplified polarity consisting of the sacred and the profane, and believes that he can have one without the other. This position won't discourage clinging, because it relies on cultivating aversion as an antidote to attraction. We can't break attachments by trying to eliminate them, because the basis of exclusion becomes selective preference. Since such selection *is* clinging, detachment arises not from keeping things out, but from letting things in.

Crazy Jane, on the other hand, has learned to take life as it is, knowing intuitively that it would be pointless to split reality into opposed preferences, as the Bishop has. What Crazy Jane offers the world is the wisdom of "bodily lowliness," a mature and loving acceptance of the ordinary human circumstance with all its inherent limits and messy contradictions. Rather than try to sort it all out, she has chosen to live with it. Crazy Jane expresses this very quality of inclusion when she tells the Bishop that "Fair *needs* foul." In doing so, she speaks a truth recognized by Buddhists everywhere: that the living Dharma is one indivisible whole, that the many are one, and that this moment, exactly as it is, is the heart's sole refuge.

THE OFTEN-TOLD TALE of two monks at a river crossing illustrates how a selective aversion invites its own opposition. The story goes that two monks came to a river crossing and found a beautiful young woman standing on the river bank, perplexed as to how to get across without soiling her shoes and clothing. One of the monks, seeing her plight, simply lifted her up in his arms and, wading into the river, carried her to the far bank. Hours and several miles later, the second monk could no longer contain his dismay over what his fellow monk had done. "We're monks," he declared. "We're not supposed to touch women. How could you pick her up like that?" His friend replied, "I set her down on the river bank, but I see that you're still carrying her."

How compelling and threatening an attraction becomes when you try to exclude its existence from your mind. If the monks wanted to be celibate and yet retain a chastity of mind, they could never hope to do so by relying on resistance alone. A chaste mind is not a mind at war with itself; a chaste mind is an undivided mind, intimate with the range of its own natural feelings and accepting of its temptations. We need to recognize when we feel angry, frightened, lustful, and so forth. But even more, we must become intimate with these feelings if we are to have any hope of acting wisely—a result that can never be achieved if we are at pains to banish anger, fear, and lust. It's only when we accept the situation as it is that these previously unwanted feelings can help us to find our way. In the end, the monk who held the living flesh in his arms remained chaste, while his traveling companion could not. His world was not split into poles of attraction and aversion, leaving him free to let things be as they are.

Since attraction and aversion are one and the same, one cannot exist without the other. The idea of the Middle Way as a safely negotiated route between polarities is a crude duality of human thought. As strange as it may seem, Buddhist equanimity is achieved not by trying to position oneself midway between extremes, but by allowing things to be as they are—extreme or not. All preference is in opposition to something, and this selectivity puts us at odds with the moment and results in lives that are habitually out of kilter.

I WAS INDISCRIMINATELY EXCITABLE as a youth, given to passionate outbursts that took hold of me in unpredictable ways. I was sometimes driven to extremes by an exaggerated sensitivity to injustice. I expected the world to be fair, and when it wasn't, I found it intolerable. Both my parents and teachers were intent on calming me down. I did my best to rid myself of the excitement that sometimes overtook me. This restraint wasn't an altogether bad approach, but it made little allowance for the possibility that my passionate faults might come to serve a valuable purpose.

At fourteen, I read John Hersey's *Hiroshima*, and I was filled with a deep sadness and a lingering sense of shame over the degree of inhumanity my species was capable of. Hersey pictured ordinary people—clerks, merchants, librarians, plumbers, teachers, and school children—who were engaged in perfectly blameless activities at the very moment the bomb descended on the city. Reading of these things, I was left with a desperate desire to make right again what had gone so terribly wrong.

The injustice of such violence weighed on me like a penance, and I began to write articles about it for the school newsletter and give talks on nonviolence for my speech class, even carrying a speech I'd written on nonviolence all the way to the national finals in a contest sponsored by the American Legion. And in private, I would tell any of my classmates who would listen the details of what happened at Hiroshima. I was driven to do these things, and to try to feel otherwise, or to feel less, was like trying to get rid of myself. I'd been given a passionate nature, a trait that went too deep to be ignored or discarded. Instead I began to regard these "excesses" as a sort of fortunate fault, and found it possible to cultivate a behavior that, though emphatic in its condemnation of violence and injustice, was more thoughtful and measured in manner. I'd finally found the restraint my parents and teachers were after, but I'd done so by way of inclusion rather than exclusion. When I quit trying to get rid of my "faults," I was given a gift that wore the sharp edges of my temperament away. I found a passionate sympathy, not only for the victims of violence but for the perpetrators as well. Like Crazy Jane, I'd learned to quit arguing with my feelings and work with them instead.

WHEN CRAZY JANE says that fair and foul are near of kin, she acknowledges that fault and virtue are intricately enfolded. Truth is known by the presence of error, courage recognized by the strength of one's fear. Furthermore, anger can serve to strengthen resolve, fear signals necessary caution, and doubt rescues one from unwarranted certainty. Before I clamp the lid down on the trashcan, I try to look first for the value in what's about to be discarded. Besides, there's something unkind in rejecting one's own nature. The Bishop's eschewing of the life he has been given exemplifies his particular ingratitude, while the "foul sty" the Bishop would have Crazy Jane discard is precisely the site of her great strength and beauty. It was there on the messy ground of her actual life that she gave birth to the love that can only be conceived in bodily lowliness. Such love is a modesty of spirit utterly unlike the pretentious purity urged by the Bishop. Crazy Jane chose to be sole and whole rather than merely intact; if this left her a little torn and broken, so be it. She didn't argue with the cost or negotiate for better terms. Without reserve, she gave herself to life completely.

In Robert Frost's poem "Birches," he writes about those times when he's "weary of considerations, and life is too much like a pathless wood":

> I'd like to get away from earth awhile
> And then come back to it and begin over,
> May no fate willfully misunderstand me
> And half grant what I wish and snatch me away
> Not to return. Earth's the right place for love:
> I don't know where it's likely to go better.

Earth *is* the right place for love, and as far as anyone knows, it's the only place. It's the place where "Fair and foul are near of kin / And fair needs foul." And if it's love you are after, then it's useless to argue with these earthly conditions. Love is not interested in spiritual ascent and makes no distinction between the sacred and profane. Love is the simple giving of oneself to circumstances without reserve or regret, and without quibbling over the consequences.

Love is a risk one takes for the sake of being fully alive.

Wu-tsu's Buffalo

ZEN MASTER WU-TSU once presented his students with an odd and troubling koan about a buffalo passing through a window. Wu-tsu said, "It is like a buffalo that passes through a latticed window. Its head, horns, and four legs all pass through. Why can't its tail pass through as well?" The image is one of a failure to pass from one circumstance to another. Were the koan illustrative of some ordinary effort at passage, say from one side of Main Street to the other, then why, when all the rest has seemingly worked its way free, can't the buffalo's tail do so as well? And since the buffalo is of a single piece one can say that if the *tail* hasn't passed through, the *buffalo* hasn't passed through. But if this image of failed passage illustrates an effort to escape the essential circumstances of the moment—perhaps to remove one's self from the worldly mundane to a higher more spiritual realm, a misadventure that many have undertaken—then it would seem that the tail knows something we'd do well to know for ourselves. If that's what the koan's about, then when Wu-tsu asks of me why the tail can't pass through, I say, "Because it's alive." And being alive, there's nowhere else for it to reside except among the living. A living tail is a handy instrument for swatting flies. The buffalo will find it useful when it discovers that the journey it has undertaken ends exactly where it began.

Wu-tsu's stymied buffalo exposes the problem of trying to get rid of something in order to *get* something. While I may disparage my life and circumstances as being too mundane, I can't squeeze myself out of my present life in order to enter any other that's better. And if "better" means something loftier, more spiritual, than having an awkward little appendage pasted to my rear, then I prize that little tail and its power to thwart escape.

When the bishop of some grand church ascends the pulpit in all his finery and religious trappings, only to inadvertently fart in his robes, what am I to make of that little impropriety? Is it understood to be opposed to the eloquent rhetoric and high purpose of his sermon? Is farting less religious, less spiritual, than not farting?

The truth is I don't know how to rank anything in accord with the presence or absence of spiritual or religious significance. I wouldn't know what to exclude, certainly not the bishop's unwitting little fart. If that were to be done away with, then why wouldn't we toss out the bishop's nose and eyes and the color of his hair as well? Why wouldn't we decry the lack of spirituality of the woman in the third row pew blowing her runny nose as delicately as she can? Why wouldn't the boy seated in the pew behind her scratching an itchy ear be judged somehow less spiritually engaged than were he kneeling for prayer? If there's some sort of distinction to be made between the mundane and the spiritual, between the worldly and the heavenly, I don't know what distinction it is, and the sooner I discard such distinctions the sooner I'll return to the birthright and blessing of ordinary life. Perhaps, like the buffalo, we have to try out the options once in order to figure this out.

Travel in Zen is circular, ending where it began. When you sign on to the Zen journey, your itinerary begins and ends in your own hometown. Alcoholics Anonymous has its own version of the futility of useless travel, which members refer to as "taking a geographical." A geographical is the effort to kick the drinking habit by changing outward locations and circumstances—moving to Albuquerque, switching girlfriends or wives, quitting your job, and so forth. AA members consider these merely outward manipulations irrelevant to addressing the inward habit itself. They like to remind each other that you can switch chairs but you're still sitting on the same old butt. Still, it's not that one must never go anywhere or change anything. It's not so much a question of whether you travel or not—it's about whether you stay home in your travels. In Zen Master Hakuin's "Song of Zazen" he writes, "Nirvana is right here, before our eyes; this very place is the Lotus Land, this very body, the Buddha." He means this reassurance to apply to wherever you happen to be. His point is that whatever the degree of your understanding, it's just what it is regardless of where you happen to reside. His encouragement is to reside exactly where you are.

Trust

I FIND MYSELF CLINGING TO BELIEFS when I don't trust myself to do otherwise. I suppose I think that if I don't come armed with a belief I won't know what to do—and the most widely held beliefs are the best because I feel shored up by the common assent of others and don't have to go it alone. The obvious irony in this is that the necessity to believe is exactly proportionate to the degree of what I don't know—and thus belief measures my failure to observe and understand. I don't "believe" in the existence of the kitchen stove or the Honda Civic parked in the garage or sunlight or gravity, or for that matter in the existence of anger, fear, and love. Such things are self-evident and can be known firsthand.

Beliefs are mental constructions designed to account for realities that can't be directly accounted for. A belief typically consists of a positive assertion regarding something that's not certain at all. It's a way we humans have of convincing ourselves that we really do know what we actually don't know. We don't tolerate loose and unaccountable realities very well and prefer to capture them in thought, regardless of how dubious such thought might be. We comfort ourselves in this way, taming the unknown by assigning it to the realm of belief. But the actual world doesn't accommodate belief very well because the world's events and values are variable and changeable, while a belief, however wise it might seem, is a static thing quickly outmoded by life's swiftness and caprice. An article of belief is a categorical generalization meant to apply to a field of specifics and thus applies intimately to none.

A tremendous capacity for harm lies in trying to force discrete events into conformity with one's beliefs. There's a complacency attendant to belief, which tends to substitute itself for continued inquiry and sustained attention. The result is neglect and self-enforced ignorance. Most public policies, both domestic and foreign, emanate from just such beliefs. And at the individual level, a predilection toward belief ensures a commensurate lack of attention. Belief invariably distracts from attending to the matter at hand.

IN THE ABSENCE OF BELIEF, we learn to trust. And what we trust is not so much any particular innate talent or wisdom of ours, but rather the living moment itself. We trust circumstances to show us what's true or more accurately to show us what's happening. And while this may seem a lot less certain than we'd like it to be, directly engaging circumstance proves to be more trustworthy than relying on ideas about circumstance. If I haven't a prepared viewpoint to guide me, then I'll be left to see for myself what's happening. And what's happening will be my best guide. This naked exposure to circumstance is what I mean by trust.

Zen literature abounds with examples of students asking for something fixed and definite to believe in, only to be turned away by their teachers. For example, it's a universal tenet of Indian Buddhism that Buddha nature pervades the whole universe, that everything *is* Buddha nature. When a monk asked Chinese Zen Master Chao-chou, "Has a dog Buddha nature or not?" Chao-chou said, "No." I have great sympathy for this monk, who only asked for confirmation of the most obvious truth, the one thing he could afford to believe in. But Chao-chou denied him. Truth is a dead thing when adopted as belief. Later, another monk tested Chao-chou with the identical question, "Has a dog Buddha nature or not?" And this time Chao-chou said, "Yes," shifting his response so that the student couldn't settle on either "Yes" *or* "No."

One irresistible attraction of belief is the hope of getting it right once and for all. And while belief itself consists of a declaration of certainty in areas of actual ignorance where no certainty is possible, people will ironically adopt beliefs to convince themselves that they've got it right. A poem by Israeli poet, Yehuda Amichai, shows the consequence of doing this:

> From the place where we are right
> Flowers will never grow
> In the spring.
> The place where we are right
> Is hard and trampled
> Like a yard.
> But doubts and loves
> Dig up the world
> Like a mole, a plow.
> And a whisper will be heard in the place
> Where the ruined house once stood.

It is the blessing of doubt to rescue me from trying to get it right. And love too of course, because love forgoes certainty in favor of sympathetic engagement. Doubt and love admit to not knowing.

When I can admit as much, I free myself to see the world as it is. I must say that there's a simple and touching appeal for me in the Zen Buddhist's willingness to enter her days in the absence of belief, asking of herself not so much about what's true or false but asking rather, "What is happening in this moment?" She has no opinion to put forth. I've learned not to acquire answers, and so hold my question open wherever I go.

Taking and Sending

*H*E'S AN OLD MAN. In his mid-nineties, I've been told. He holds on to the handrail and descends shakily, one deliberate step at a time, into the water of Chico Creek where it's dammed up at Sycamore Pool. He comes here nearly every morning during the summer months to cool off. Today he's wearing swim shorts and a T-shirt, but at other times I've seen him walk into the water with his street clothes on, even his shoes. Once in the water, he doesn't swim but walks slowly toward the deeper end of the pool until the water rises to his chin. Then he turns about and makes his way back to the pool steps. He moves so slowly as to make his progress nearly imperceptible, and the journey takes a good while to complete. I've watched him there where he climbs up out of the pool and more or less collapses on a poolside bench, the weight of gravity pulling down on his old bones. And at such times, I feel the strain of his effort and, though I'm going on seventy-five years myself, I'd trade bodies with him for a while if I could and give him a day off from the difficulty his life has become. He constantly "nibbles" his lips, as though he were always chewing on something, yet when I speak with him, he's perfectly clear in what he says and understands.

One morning the old man asked me if I cooked for myself, and I told him that I did. "I have a housekeeper," he said. "She cooks for me, but it's mostly sandwiches." He seemed unhappily resigned to this circumstance, but I felt the weight of his hunger for something else to eat as though I too were limited to a diet of sandwiches.

IT'S NOT UNUSUAL of course that we humans suffer in these ways—and it's not unusual to feel sympathy for another and want to relieve his distress. In fact, the sympathetic frame of mind that arose in me that day where the old man sat dripping water has a formal counterpart in the Buddhist practice of *tonglen*. Tonglen is sometimes called the "compassion breath." It's a practice of Tibetan Buddhism and was popularized in the West by Chögyam Trungpa. Tonglen is sometimes referred to as "doing the exchange" or of "taking and sending." The idea in tonglen is to imagine yourself literally breathing in the suffering of another regardless of how painful it might be, and to breathe out in exchange whatever comfort you have to offer.

If, for example, I should come upon a particularly insulting and hurtful argument between two people, I breathe the hurt and the insult into my own body and I breathe out whatever kindness or calm I can give to the situation. In other words I take in what I don't want and give away what I want, which makes tonglen a powerful practice of inclusion, a practice in not looking away, in staying in the circumstance no matter how unpleasant or threatening the circumstance might at the moment be. Tonglen is not a game. One must be truly willing to take on another's pain and distress.

In practice, tonglen is a frontal assault on the defenses of the ego-self. Ego is a tenuous construction of thought, and therefore vulnerable to counter-thought. Because of its contrived nature, ego can't allow even the slightest doubt to threaten the credibility of its own self-view, sustaining itself by a more or less constant vigilance against the mental infiltration of discordant contradiction. Ego's defensive strategy is one of entertaining only those thoughts favorable to its continuation, admitting what serves this purpose and excluding what doesn't, subsisting entirely on the basis of acknowledging only what's wanted and studiously ignoring what isn't. The practice of tonglen, with its pattern of taking and sending, reverses this situation and thereby defeats ego's essential strategy.

In defending its worth, ego depends on the tactic of favorably comparing itself to others, a sort of "I'm glad I'm not like that!" perception of the world. Such a tactic, one so selective with its sympathies, forfeits the capacity for compassionate response. If I'm unwilling to identify with who you happen to be and what you happen to be doing or experiencing, I lose the essential basis for empathic understanding. Tonglen offers a way out of such self-imprisoning incapacity and teaches one how to relate to the suffering of others.

WITH THE CONTINUED PRACTICE OF TONGLEN, the division marking the boundary of self and other falls away and your person and situation becomes my person and situation. And when that happens, I move beyond isolated identity and awaken to the radically integrated identity of all beings, human and otherwise, sentient and non-sentient. In 1976, a poem by Native American activist Ila Abernathy was published in *Akwesasne Notes* that speaks to this awakening:

I am grass growing and the shearer of grass,
I am the willow and the splitter of laths,
weaver and the thing woven,
marriage of willow and grass.
I am frost on the land and the land's life,
breath and beast and the sharp rock underfoot;
in me the mountain lives, and the owl strikes,
and I in them. I am the sun's twin,
mover of blood, and the blood lost,
I am the deer and the deer's death;
I am the burr in your conscience:
acknowledge me.

If I am "the sun's twin," am I not as well twin to the shopper with a package in hand crossing the intersection at Fifth and Broadway, the father picking his daughter up at Chico High, the nurse at Enloe Hospital fitting an IV to the arm of a patient, an old man at Sycamore Pool wishing for something to eat not found between two slices of bread?

While it might seem strange to lose the little separate person I have mistaken myself to be and find myself dispersed into my surroundings in this way, it's a loss that sets isolated longing to rest. Compassion breath is a journey of will into the heart of another only to find there your own heart, which is all our hearts.

This or That

THE PROBLEM WITH DUALISTIC THINKING is that it offers the mind so few options—two in fact. And what's more, these two options are typically regarded as mutually exclusive of each other. Supposedly you either you get *this* or you get *that*, but never both or neither—and certainly never all four! Dualistic thinking assumes a world of binary antagonisms. It's a particularly violent frame of mind in which every object, person, event, or circumstance is comprised of opposition.

Walking in the park this morning, I came upon a young father lifting his boy of three or four years out of a stroller. The boy, bored with being pushed in the stroller, wanted to push it himself. I said to the father, "Looks like you're getting some help." And then I said to the boy, "You can push for a while and let daddy ride." I was just being chatty, feeling expansive and happy. But the young father had a point to make and said to me, "You're either a pusher in this world or you get pushed on." And then he added, "You're never too young to learn that." I was taken aback a little by the sense he'd made of his boy's wanting to help out, and I asked, "Couldn't it be a matter of sometimes you get a ride and sometimes give a ride?" But even with the suggestion of that gentle alternative, I saw his jaw set in disagreement to the idea that the world was anything other than a place in which either you shove people around or you get shoved around. It's a viewpoint that necessitates securing the advantage, an argument for preemptive attack.

A persistent perception of the world as competing oppositions arises from falsely and invariably viewing mutual exclusion as mutual antagonism rather than as complement. We all learn that water and oil don't mix, but that fact doesn't necessitate the conclusion that the two are somehow at odds with each other. Every bite of apple or orange or handful of nuts or slice of bread you've ever swallowed contains both oil and water, each essential to your health. I'm not claiming that forces never collide, or that there's never a time to shove back if someone's pushing you around. What I am saying is that apparent opposites often comprise a creative synergy, the way bookends paired in just proportion oppose one another so that each is held upright, or the way the mortar complements the pestle by its very resistance, or how the self-same force that throws the wave up shore draws it down again.

FOR ZEN STUDENTS, the point at which forces exert themselves on one another is a point of crucial turning. What do you do when someone's intent on shoving you around? Acknowledging the impulse to shove back, the Zen student can choose not to. Even the tiniest gap between provocation and response is an opportunity to redirect the force of harmful karma toward a more peaceful outcome. The best response to someone who wants to shove you around may be to simply give ground. The bully wants a fight; the arguer, an argument. What alternative might they turn to when they fail to provoke the reaction they're looking for? An insult that's absorbed without complaint loses its force and disappoints the insulter. Yielding turns the Dharma wheel back toward modesty and kindness, offering to others an option that's often overlooked.

There's harmony at work in every apparent contrast, a reciprocal exchange that equates with the Buddha's doctrine of *paticca samupadda*, dependent origination. "This being, that becomes; from the arising of this, that arises; this not being, that becomes not; from the ceasing of this, that ceases." The truth of the teaching lies in the fact that the perception of *this* and *that* as separable entities is false. Nothing that exists is independently autonomous.

As Joanna Macy puts it, "There is a mutuality here, a reciprocal dynamic. Power inheres not in any entity, but in the relationship between entities." Opposition vanishes when perception shifts from entity to relationship, from object to movement. In physics, matter and energy are seen as interchangeable, energy manifesting as matter, matter manifesting as energy. Our seemingly disparate human lives are linked together with the same necessity as breathing in is linked with breathing out. You and I are one body, not two.

Verbal opposition, such as *near* and *far*, *high* and *low*, *wide* and *narrow*, is embedded in language to such an extent that one can say that language itself is constructed of opposition. Opposition is a necessary characteristic of language for the very reason that it's a part of the very nature of thought. "This or that" serves as an intellectual tool for navigating ungovernable realities that are otherwise incomprehensible. But such oppositional language, however necessary to thought it may be, is nonetheless arbitrary in the same manner in which mathematical "language" is arbitrary, its "truth" or "accuracy" lying wholly within its own finite parameters.

Language is merely expressive of its own oppositional form, its truth or logic is that of subject and predicate, grammar and lexicon.

To a great extent, language is a system closed off within itself; the logic of language merely confirms the logic of language. If I account for this, I can utilize language the way I might use a yardstick, for example, to measure the width of a door, recognizing the inches and feet and even "width" itself to be ideas about reality and not reality itself. In this way, language, like a clock or a set of measuring spoons, becomes a useful instrument. In the same way, words like *near* and *far* are a useful means of comprehension and communication, in so far as I don't confuse them with the seamless continuum of space itself. In a very real sense, *near* and *far* is not a matter of *this* or *that*, but rather a measurement of a single undivided distance.

THE OPPOSITIONAL NATURE of language lends itself to intolerance and exclusion. Polarities like *good* and *evil*, *sacred* and *profane*, *beautiful* and *ugly* bear with them an emotional persuasion that lures the unwary toward a mind entrapped by irreconcilable opposites. It's the dualistic nature of such a persuasion that brings one to perceive even life and death as antagonists divided against each other, rather than as one complementary expression of a single creation.

It's not that people and events don't ever rub up against each other or that life is never without conflict. It's just that these rough spots are only bumps in a long, long road and may serve to slow the traffic down. I wonder if the young father's philosophy of *push and shove* is that much at odds with my own view of *give and get a ride*. Perhaps, after all, our contrasting views are more complimentary than opposed. He wants his boy to recognize competition when it arises and know when to take an opponent on. I'd like the boy to recognize cooperation as well, and know when to offer a hand.

I'm glad I didn't argue the point.

Storing the Broom

I DON'T CARE MUCH FOR RULES. I'll follow them if need be, but I seldom make them up on my own.

When I first went to train at a Zen monastery, I was instructed in a fair number of precise procedures, rituals, and behaviors that I was expected to comply with in detailed and exacting ways. The resident monks seemed quite earnest about these rules and were studious in insisting on their implementation. I couldn't, for example, get up early and go to the zendo to sit zazen, because I'd been explicitly ordered to stay in bed until the morning gong was rung. And when I finally got to the zendo, there were numerous ritualistic moves required of me. I must enter the zendo through the left half of the open doorway, taking care to put the right foot across the threshold first, then take two more steps into the room, stop and bow, proceed clockwise around the room to my cushion, bow to the cushion, and so forth. I must never turn my back on the altar. I mustn't read a novel, magazine, or any literature other than the official "spiritual" literature available in the monastery's guest bookshelves—and even then only during the forty minutes desig-nated for spiritual reading. There was nothing one did in the monastery, not a single activity, including relieving oneself at the toilet or taking a shower, to which there was not a required ritual behavior attached. The source of inspiration for the monastery's complex rules of behavior was Dogen Zenji's comprehensive regu-lations set down centuries before.

What I did with all these rules while in the monastery was to apply myself to them. I didn't ask whether they were agreeable to me or not. Instead I determined that I would do what was asked of me and see what I might learn from relinquishing virtually all autonomy. What would it be like to have little or no control over either my time or my actions?

As a result, I soon discovered how much I wanted to have things my own way. I remember in particular a time when I was set to building a set of storage shelves in the monastery's wood shop. I was within five minutes of completing the job when the gong signal-ing the end of work meditation rang. Everything in the monastery was regulated to a precise time, and when the gong sounded, I was expected to drop what I was doing and go immediately to the next scheduled activity. But with just one more saw cut and a dozen nails hammered down, I could put the last shelf in place and the two-hour job would be properly finished. I scribed a line on a shelving board and was about to carry it to the saw, when the shop foreman, a senior monk, gestured to me to drop the work and leave. "But I'm just minutes from being done," I complained. "The work medita-tion period is over," was all he said.

Complying with the rules was a valuable teaching for me. Of course, it took a while for its positive implications to sink in, but in time I was able to curb some of the resistance I felt regarding any seeming intrusion into my own self-willed control over my time and activities. And even more importantly, I began to realize that the comparative autonomy I imagined was mine outside the monastery was a delusion. I'd never been free to do as I wished. I'd only struggled to be so, a defense against interference that exacted from me an exhausting degree of resistance. Even today I sometimes hear the monastery gong, its insistence reaching me through the intervening years, telling me I'm needed elsewhere. When the call comes and I'm at some task of my own choosing, I remember to drop what I'm doing and respond.

But the observance of Zen rules and rituals also has a potential to become obsessive, leading individuals to cling to arbitrary forms as an indispensable concomitant to Zen practice. Hold your thumbs just right or your zazen's no good. In its extreme, adherence to form is mistaken for Zen itself and becomes the student's major religious focus. This approach forfeits the path of Zen altogether. Not uncommonly, disputes about such matters arise within various sanghas, threatening the cohesion and stability of the group. In one sangha, the two resident roshis, both of whom were talented writers, introduced a revised version of the four bodhisattva vows, triggering a great outcry from alarmed members, one of whom said to me, "It just isn't right. Some things shouldn't be tampered with."

On another occasion, I could never get clear instructions on the ritual of opening and closing the zendo, a ritual involving the presentation of the *kyosaku*. Having gone to the altar and taken up the kyosaku, was I then to circle the zendo clockwise first and counterclockwise second, or counterclockwise first and clockwise second? I felt foolish even inquiring about such a thing. But then, after all, when the time came for me to perform the ritual, I'd be faced with having to walk one direction or the other. I couldn't get clear instructions on this matter, because neither the roshis nor the

Sensei nor the Head of Practice could agree on how the thing was to be done. There was a faction among them who complained that the way the sangha had been previously doing it was "not the way they do it in Japan." That apparently carried some weight with the others, especially those who couldn't claim firsthand knowledge of Japanese Zen ritual. I was eventually handed detailed written instructions on the ritual of opening and closing the zendo as set down in the sangha manual, but when I followed these official instructions, I was told that I'd done it wrong.

I was never able to open and close the zendo to the satisfaction of all the involved parties; if one person was pleased another was not. And so I was obliged to be content with doing it "wrong." I thought it was good for me to be in such a circumstance. There's something about doing the best you can while knowing it won't be right that takes the stiffness out of one's spine and softens the hard edges of ambition and intent. At the very least I was moved toward a more informed sympathy for others who can't get it right. I discovered a nearly exact counterpart to my own failures in a Zen koan about a monk named Ma-ku. It's told that "Ma-ku, carrying his ring staff, went to Ch'ang-ch'ing. He circled the meditation seat three times, then shook his staff once and stood there upright. Ch'ang-ch'ing said, 'Right! Right!' Ma-ku also went to Nan-ch'uan: he circled the meditation seat three times, shook his staff once and stood there upright. Nan-ch'uan said, 'Wrong! Wrong!'" I have an understanding sympathy for Ma-ku when, bewildered, he complained to Nan-ch'uan, "Ch'ang ch'ing said 'Right.' Why do you say 'Wrong,' Master?" Ma-ku's situation, like my own, offers the optimal circumstance for discouraging perfectionism.

I once had a teacher, Reverend Master Jiyu Kennett, who was a stickler on doing rituals right. She wrote books of detailed instructions on every little move for all the basic Buddhist services conducted at the monastery. Yet, when she herself performed these rituals, she often got them wrong, failing to accord with her own instructions. But whatever she did wrong was done by her with such a veritable dignity of error that wrong seemed the only right way to do it. I admired her for that, and have tried to follow her lead, opening and closing the zendo in full command of the wrong way, gracing error with all the dignity I can muster.

A heightened concern for getting the forms right is perhaps the most pernicious, contagious, and persistent malady to overtake Zen students, distracting them from what actually matters. It's epidemic among some of the most serious and promising of students, who in trying to get everything right, get nothing right. In Shunyru Suzuki's biography, *Crooked Cucumber*, an incident is told involving a student who is described as "always trying to be a model student, fanatically attempting to do everything right, and tripping over himself in the process." One evening when Suzuki had just finished giving a talk at Tassajara Zen Center, this student asked Suzuki if Tassajara shouldn't have more rules like monasteries in Japan. He went on to complain that at Tassajara "some people were using the baths outside the scheduled time," and that too much talking was going on. Suzuki obliged the student by giving him a rule. A broom was standing in a corner of the room, and Suzuki said, "Ah, see that broom over there? It's standing on its bristles. That's not good for the broom. The bristles will bend, and it won't work so well or last so long. There—that's a good rule."

What I like most about Suzuki's rule to store the broom with the bristles up is that it's embedded in the affairs of ordinary life to a degree that resists distinction as a specifically Zen rule. And for that very reason, it's as Zen a rule as you'll ever find. Besides, it's good for the broom. I'd like to think that it was good as well for the anxious student to whom the rule was given.

Not everyone who faithfully observes Zen procedures is obsessive in doing so. For such students, there is nothing indispensable about the particular forms they practice. They just do what they were taught to do without giving it much thought one way or another. When they hold incense, they hold it in their hands and not in their thoughts and they light it with an ordinary match without artificially elevating the act with sentiments of spiritual significance. For these students, the precision and repetition of ritual is a practice in simple mindfulness, noticing and being present in what they do. In this way, the disembodied mind returns to the body until mind and body are indistinguishable and both drop out of sight. Thus, ritual generates itself: bowing does the bowing and zazen does zazen and chant becomes a movement entirely of the throat and tongue and lips. The universe moves on its own and it's not the student's concern to interfere. It is then that every act of rule or ritual is just another storing of the broom with the bristles turned upward.

Enter from There

T HE STORY GOES that a monk named Ching-ch'ing came
to Zen Master Hsuan-sha seeking instruction. Ching-
ch'ing said, "I've come seeking the truth. Please, master, tell
me how I can enter the way of Zen." Hsuan-sha said, "Can you hear
the sound of the creek down beyond the gate?" Ching-ch'ing listened, and replied, "Yes, master, I can hear it." "Enter Zen from
there," Hsuan-sha told him.

I can better understand the nature of Ching-ch'ing's question
when I consider it in the light of Zenkei Shibayama's distinction
between the Zen School of Buddhism and Zen itself. In his book,
A Flower Does Not Talk, Shibayama writes, "Zen can be accepted as
Zen itself, or the Truth itself, apart from its narrow sectarian interpretation as a school of Buddhism. When Zen is seen in such a
broad sense, Zen means the Truth, or the Absolute; it is not limited
to Buddhism alone, but is the basis of all religions and all philosophies." And to this I would add that Zen in that broader sense is the
basis of all sciences and literature as well. Zen itself has as its

referent reality itself, the way things are. Zen is simply a word denoting what actually exists, what is. No religious tradition, philosophy, science, or literary movement has a monopoly on "truth" of that sort.

I think that's the sort of broader truth Ching-ch'ing came seeking. If he were asking about the school of Zen, he would have checked in with the monastery's head monk and asked what he needed to do to join the sangha. What Ching-ch'ing is after is Zen itself, and that's what Hsuan-sha gave him. He turned Ching-ch'ing away from whatever sort of explanatory teaching he might have anticipated and handed him back to the living moment itself. To enter Zen is to enter your own life, which can only be done from exactly where you are. If you feel lost or confused or worried, enter from there. If you are happy or sad or angry or frightened or elated, enter from there. If your zazen is lousy or the best you've ever had, enter from there. If you've just lost your job or been promoted to vice president of the firm, enter from there. Pema Chödrön, one of the most compassionate and realistic of all Buddhist teachers, has written a whole book, *Start Where You Are*, based on the necessity of doing just that.

There's a transparent wisdom in the advice to start where you are, the joke being that you can't really do otherwise. It's an obvious requisite of any navigational operation. But where is it that you are? It's a question worth asking oneself, because we humans are given to constructing storied itineraries of our lives, a habit that makes our reports of our imagined whereabouts of doubtful accuracy. If you have mistaken, as Ching-ch'ing apparently had, the true location of your starting point, you can't actually start to move on from where you are.

I LEARNED SOMETHING about this firsthand many years ago when I was teaching college literature. A Selection Committee had been formed to pick someone from among the faculty to represent the Humanities Division at an educational policy forum held by the Dean of Education. After the committee's deliberations, I and many others in the Humanities Division were dismayed to hear that a certain D.C. had been chosen for the post. D.C. actually had a name, but among his other eccentricities, he was certain to correct any one who called him by his full name, insisting that he be called D.C. He was also given to telling jokes that were so odd or sometimes silly that none of us could quite catch the humor D.C. saw in them. He'd sit in faculty meetings, offering nothing to the proceedings and then inappropriately break in with one of his jokes. He seldom showed any interest in the issues under consideration. In private, my conversations with D.C. consisted of "Did you hear the one about . . ." or a tedious analysis of his golf swing. But to tell the truth, I liked D.C. There was something innocent and boyish about him that appealed to me, but I couldn't imagine him in any situation that required thoughtful consideration and judgment. He didn't appear to have any of the qualities he would need to start with.

I was serving as the English Department chairperson at the time, and the department's representation to the Education Dean was critical to the English program. So I got hold of Margaret Kinney, who'd chaired the Selection Committee, and asked how they'd come to pick D.C. "He really wanted the job," she said. "He was the senior applicant. Aside from telling him he wasn't competent, we had no other reason to pass him by in favor of someone else." The Humanities Dean, Ron Menmuir, had to give final authorization for D.C.'s appointment, so I took my worries to him. I laid it all out to Ron about how we had seven departments in the Humanities Division and we needed a strong candidate to represent us. "He's going to be involved in making policy," I said. "If he gets it wrong, we're all hurting."

"Has he ever asked to do something like this before?" Ron inquired.

"Not that I know of."

"Now he has," Ron said.

And that was a fact. D.C. had just done something none of us had ever known him to do before. He'd asked to help.

"He's got to start with what he's got," Ron said. "I could give D.C. a job shrunk down to his apparent size or see if he can grow to the size of the one he's asked for."

It hadn't been long, less than a year, since I'd awakened in a rented room at the rear of some stranger's house, my marriage effectively ended. It took a minute that first morning to remember where I was and that the house I'd lived in for eighteen years was no longer mine to call home. Everything in my new surroundings was alien to me, and it seemed inconceivable that I had no option but to get out of bed and begin my day from the cramped unfamiliarity of this rented room. Aside from a few personal items and the clothes occupying the half closet I'd been allotted, nothing in that room had anything to do with me. And even now, months later, talking to Ron Menmuir in his office at the college, I was still commuting to work from a sixteen-foot travel trailer parked on a ridge south of town. Okay, I thought, if I can start a day's work from that makeshift campsite I now call home, then maybe D.C. can start his new job from the science of a golf swing and a repertoire of puzzling jokes. We enter our lives from where we are whether it's my turn or D.C.'s. When I left Ron's office that day, D.C. was my representative to the Dean and I'd decided to help him in any way I could.

REGARDLESS OF HOW FORTUNATE OR UNFORTUNATE my circumstance may appear to me, it's the only place from which I can enter the next moment of my life. Even the worst of situations offers its own peculiar strength, courage, and insight to guide and support me in taking the next step. Starting where I am depends on accepting where I am. It depends as well on accepting *who* I am. Nothing but this unqualified honesty ever works, because if I fabricate my situation and person, if I lie to myself in these ways, I forfeit my one and only life in favor of opting for a pointless fiction. If I want to live in the truth of Zen, I must call my true self into being each moment of my life. This is the only truth available.

Sometime after Hsuan-sha told Ching-ch'ing to enter Zen from the sound of the creek, a visiting scholar named Yang'k'uei related the exchange to Master An of Hsien-yen. Yang'k'uei wanted to know what would have happened if Ching-ch'ing had not heard the sound of the creek. "If Hsuan-sha couldn't tell Ching-ch'ing to enter from there," Yang-k'uei wondered, "how then, would Hsuan-sha have told Ching-ch'ing to enter Zen?" An suddenly called out, "Professor!" Without thought Yang k'uei answered, "Yes, Master." An said, "Enter Zen from there."

Chinese Zen master Jui-yen entered his life every day in just this manner. Jui-yen would call out to himself, "Oh Master!" and would answer himself, "Yes?" "Are you awake?" he would ask, and would answer, "Yes, I am." "Never be deceived by others, any day, any time." "No, I won't." Jui-yen's daily conversation with himself demonstrates the degree to which entering Zen is a matter of answering the call when you're called for. "Are you awake?" he asks himself.

"Am I awake?" I ask myself. Am I willing to show up in my own person and be who I am and start from where I am? The question is critical because if I don't start from the reality of my actual being and circumstance, the very first step will be false and I'm certain to stumble. So to enter Zen, I need to be willing to be myself and work with what I've got. And this in turn requires that I see myself as I am.

The Zen word for doing this is "mindfulness," but "mindfulness" somehow conjures up a project of some sort, a specialized religious effort of a kind. Mindfulness tends to become too much a thing in its own right, whereas what I'm recommending is a simple matter of paying attention. Attention to what? Attention to whatever I'm thinking, saying, or doing at the moment. To pay attention in this way is to enter Zen. It's an affectionate behavior, a kindness, the gift of yourself given to yourself. When the call comes, and the call comes all the time, "Oh Master! Oh Kirk! Oh Susan! Oh Lin! Oh whoever!" can I, like Jui-yen of old, answer, "Yes, I'm here."

But I still need to ask who's calling. Who is this master that calls? And who is it that answers? And is the one who answers different or the same as the one who calls? Is Jui-yen's conversation between two or one? When the call comes, is it my voice I hear calling? Is it my voice that answers? It is here that one truly enters Zen, here where the voice of the creek is the one voice that exists, and where no one's voice, however distinctive, is merely his own. We enter Zen from the particular, knowing that the particular is Zen itself, so that Zen is everywhere and everything at once. You and I dwell where the wind speaks the language of our hearts, where sea wave and bird's song and child's laughter speaks the language of our hearts. We find our voice each day in words the universe utters.

Molting

*I*T WAS A TINY FEATHER, not more than an inch and a half in length, pale gray and barely discernible against the matching gray surface of the sidewalk. And then there was a second feather as well. It's unlikely that I'd have noticed them at all if a little breeze hadn't blown them about just as I came along. This was in mid-August, and the House Sparrows that nest in the hollows and crevices under the eaves of the building that houses Chico Natural Foods were beginning their fall molt from breeding plumage into their winter feathers.

Most birds molt once or twice a year and for a variety of reasons, the most common being to replace old worn feathers. But they may also molt from a lighter summer plumage into a heavier plumage in cold areas where they intend to stay on through the winter. In addition birds molt in and out of breeding plumage, and adolescent birds molt into their adult feathers. Molts can enact quite startling transformations. The little male ruddy duck, for example, common to North America, is a rather nondescript bird in its winter plumage, brownish overall with pale sides, a slightly darkened cap and white cheeks being its most distinguishing features. But when it molts into breeding plumage, its whole body turns a deep ruddy color and its large flat bill converts from a rather drab gray to a brilliant, luminous blue, its contrasting white cheeks flashing on and off with every turn of its head like mirrors deflecting the sun.

I don't know how a Ruddy Duck, or any other bird for that matter, experiences the occasion of these sometimes radically transforming molts. First they're one sort of bird and then they're quite another. Do they realize this? Does the little Ruddy Duck realize his own sudden brilliance when he emerges into breeding plumage or feel dimmed when he reverts once again to his ordinary winter feathers?

I, too, have been losing a lot of "feathers" these days, and I *do* notice the change. Little bits of me are dropping away—worn out thoughts, ideas, beliefs, and certainties. Sometimes whole identities drop away, along with a world I thought I once knew.

The mechanism for a molt is that the old, worn feathers are loosened in their follicles by the growth of new intruding feathers, which eventually push them out. I'm aware that what is being pushed out is "me" but have as yet no clear awareness of what's coming to take my place. I've had other molts in my long life, some more dramatic than others, but none more comprehensive, more thorough, than what's occurring now. Zen is a practice that self-destructs, disappears in order to become what it is. I'm seventy-five years old as I write this. I've been a teacher of Zen for years, yet when people ask me if I'm a Buddhist, I don't know what to say. Any answer I might give somehow seems irrelevant to what's actually taking place. I've lost any convincing identification and seem to be a prospect for a missing persons alert. It's as if I've awakened to the company of a stranger, or as if I've reached out at last and taken hold of my own unfamiliar hand.

The molting of birds can be either sudden or gradual. The sudden or synchronous molters change their feathers all at once in a period as short as two weeks. Waterfowl typically do this, and are unable to fly until the molt is complete, leaving them exposed and vulnerable for the duration. Other birds molt in stages, dropping their feathers in a pattern that allows them to sustain flight throughout the adaptation. These variants of the molt seem to me particularly analogous and expressive of what Zen calls "awakening"—the self losing itself in order to realize itself, the self settling into itself, awakening to what it truly is. It's an awakening that might come with the startling suddenness of brilliant new feathers or arrive in increments, one feather at a time, in a transformation so subtle as to be nearly indiscernible until complete.

Awakening may result in radically altered plumage but the crucial insight, the actual enlightenment, is not so much about getting new feathers as it is about being stripped of the old. Awakening is within the interim between molts when what you were before has passed away and what you are to become is not yet realized. Awakening arises in times of vulnerability and awkwardness between before and after where prior identities are cancelled and anything is possible and nothing certain. It is in that place of no-place and in that "person" of no particularity that you come closest to the source of all feathers and to the act of feathering itself. You are the very expression of the follicle, the vehicle and container, wherein the drama of the molt itself is being enacted.

Birds have no option but to trust the molt to do its work; indeed, the renewal and perpetuation of all species of birds absolutely depends upon its occurrence. In like manner we humans are overtaken by change, and we do well to entrust ourselves to its care. I may not have desired any change at all or see any particular need for it, but the continuing transformation goes on regardless, and has gone on the whole of my life whether I choose to acknowledge it or not.

On the sidewalk outside Chico Natural Foods, I watched one day as two tiny gray feathers drifted over the curb edge and into the street. The stoplight turned to green once more and the traffic flowed through and the feathers were lost to sight. And I too was lost to sight, saying goodbye once more to whoever I'd once been, drifting along like a loosened feather on its way to who knows where. Overhead, House Sparrows, their nesting season finished, were hopping about in the sycamores the city had planted there.

Ten Thousand Mistakes

THERE'S LITTLE OF BUDDHIST LITURGY OR RITUAL these days that I find indispensable. Still, I follow a daily pattern of chanting the Heart Sutra, a praise for Avalokiteshvara, the Three Refuges, and the bodhisattva vows, along with the traditional bowing and ringing of the gong. I couldn't tell you why I continue to do so. I think I once had reasons but if so I've forgotten what the reasons were. I no longer ask why I'm doing any of this or feel any need to know. I just do what I was once taught to do—and none of it feels essential.

It's ironic that the one element of Buddhist liturgy that I *do* find indispensable is not among those I observe daily. I entered the path of Zen because I was weary of the hurt and pain I somehow managed to cause myself and others, and I thought that Zen might help me to cease from it. The truth is I felt guilty. Old wrongs of mine would rise up in memory, prior events of sometimes forty or fifty years earlier, and I would cringe at the recollection, feeling lost beyond the possibility of forgiveness. It's puzzling to me what sorts of memories come to haunt me in this way, seemingly minor lapses in kindness that might seem insignificant to others but somehow loom large among the things I wish I hadn't done.

ONE INCIDENT THAT RETURNS to trouble me occurred fifty-three years ago as I write this. A draftee, I was stationed at the Presidio in San Francisco on my way to an assignment overseas. While there I met Malaya, a Filipina woman of thirty years or so who'd lost a husband through separation or death—I never bothered to find out which, though she spoke of him often. Malaya and I liked each other and spent a lot of time together. Neither of us had much money and so we took walks along the waterfront and sat at benches in the park. I sometimes took advantage of my option to include a guest at the Presidio mess hall in order to save us the cost of a meal, and Malaya got us in to free movies at the theater where she worked shifts at the ticket counter. And when we felt like treating ourselves, we'd share a steaming bowl of *cioppino*, Italian fish stew, at a little North Beach restaurant, sitting together at the counter with paper bibs hung about our necks, wiping our hands on terry cloth towels still warm from the dryer.

Malaya was thin and angular with dark hair and large brown eyes. She was alternately playful and pensive. She'd invariably cry over the sad parts in the movies we saw. She'd take off in a sudden run when we walked in the park, like a child playing hide-and-go-seek. She had two prominent gold fillings that flashed in the light when she smiled or laughed. My buddies at the Presidio liked her as much as I did and nicknamed her "Skinny Gold," which made her laugh and show her fillings all the more. Malaya rented a small room in the Pacific Heights district and at length she told me she was allowed visitors in her room and I could be the first. She hadn't had any "visitors" at all for a long time she said. But telling me this, she seemed pretty excited about the prospect now. She could get a friend to trade shifts at the theater and we could meet at her room the next afternoon. "Am I being too bold?" she asked. "Now don't run off," she said. "It'll be fun. You'll see. I'll bring some flowers."

But I did run off. I said I'd be there and then I wasn't. To this day, I can't say why I did that—except that I liked her so much that I was unnerved by the prospect of further intimacy. Perhaps I didn't want to be closer than we already were. I'd recently suffered a painful breakup that had left me fearful and guarded. I hadn't told Malaya about this, and even then when she'd invited me further into her life and I needed to be candid with her, I couldn't bring myself to tell her how I felt. I left her that day with the impression that we would meet the next afternoon. Afterward, I avoided the places where we were likely to meet, and was soon shipped overseas. I think Malaya probably had misgivings of her own, and might have chosen me as a partner because she knew I'd soon be sent overseas. But to this day, the thought of Malaya getting off work early and coming home to her apartment with a grinning mouth full of gold and a fist full of flowers only to find out she'd been stood up still breaks my heart.

IT IS JUST SUCH FAILURES of honesty and loving-kindness that carry for me the heaviest sense of wrong—how I once injured a high-school teammate, showing off my physical prowess in football practice; how I provoked Ms. Talbot to tears in front of the whole senior English class, the one teacher who'd looked beyond my behavior and found talent she'd hoped to promote; how I repaid the kindness and support of the plant foreman at Rinshed Mason Automotive Paints by abruptly quitting without giving notice.

Burdened with the pain of such memories, I asked my Zen teachers for help. Among the things they gave me was a contrition verse:

> All the ancient twisted karma
> From beginningless greed, hatred, and ignorance
> Born of my body, mouth, and thought
> I now confess openly and fully.

From that day to this, whenever I feel like a thoroughly bad person, I chant this simple confession. The chanting is an offering to those I've wronged, persons who have since died or whose whereabouts are lost to me and to whom I can no longer make direct amends. Even if Malaya or Ms. Talbot or the shop foreman can't know in person how sorry I am, there's still something about the wholehearted admittance of wrongdoing that softens the hard edge of guilt. The words of contrition drop like tears that come unbidden, and a tender and regretful remorse arises, a sorrow for whatever harm has been brought by my doings. It is this exposed heart of sorrow, vulnerable and unguarded, that heals the wound of guilt and allows for sympathy and forgiveness to do their work.

I'd had the contrition verse in my keeping for some time before I became curious about the word *beginningless*. How is it, I wondered, that greed, hatred, and ignorance are said to be *beginningless*?

In time, I came to see that I hadn't personally invented my own wrongdoings. They came ready-made for my use, and in fact the whole human catalogue of potential wrongs was an inheritance. The "ancient twisted karma" of the contrition verse was a vast impersonal stream into which I'd been cast at birth. The genesis of greed, hatred, and ignorance was itself unknown, lost in antiquity and impossible to imagine. The potential for wrongdoing must have been present before the birth of the universe itself, an option for harm that we humans fell heir to. And the same must be true of generosity, love, and wisdom, which were always here and for which I can claim no individual merit or lack of it.

But that doesn't absolve me of responsibility.

I can choose, and it is this exercise of volition, an equally ancient potential of human behavior, that holds me accountable for the consequences of what I do. While I did not set in motion the karmic stream, it's nonetheless up to me how I negotiate its currents. I can go with the current, swim against it, or seek a shoreline, but the currents and eddies of the stream are forever shifting and leave me no option but to continually decide what to do. My choices bear upon the stream itself, for it is, as I said, an impersonal stream and therefore a mutual stream in which all of creation swims. I can do nothing that will not affect you. You can do nothing that will not affect me. We are awash together, bound in such intricate and binding reciprocity that if anything moves, all the rest moves with it.

AN OLD CHINESE STORY tells of a monk who came to Zen Master Ta-sui with a question about a teaching he'd gotten from a traditional Buddhist cosmology telling of a conflagration that sweeps through at the end of the eon and totally destroys the universe. This disastrous prophecy is a metaphor of consequence carried out on a colossal, universal scale. In the face of universal destruction, the monk wonders, "Is *this* destroyed or not?"

Ta-sui said, "It is destroyed."

The monk said, "If so, then *this* goes along with it."

Ta-sui said, "It goes along with it."

Perhaps the monk thought that something could be salvaged, not carried along in the otherwise universal sweep of events. He wonders if there is something exempt from the common conflagration.

Ta-sui tells him that it all goes together. The exchange touches the wistful heart of that moment where life spills into emptiness and the monk says for himself, "If so, then *this* goes along with it."

I suppose every heartbeat is the end of an eon wherein whatever the moment is goes along with it. The consequence of my morning's remark to my neighbor on his way to work will be carried along to who knows where? Perhaps he will carry the sense of what I said to another and from there it will radiate from person to person as they touch each other's lives throughout the day. Maybe my neighbor himself will carry it with him to lunch and haul it back home again after work. Perhaps he'll return it to me some day. Or, perhaps he'll leave it right where I said it this morning, and it will go nowhere else at all. The dispersal of consequence is without known limit, as endless as the verse says it is beginningless. It's not hard to imagine that my casual morning comment to my neighbor, wishing him a good day, may some day go streaming among the stars on its dark flight toward destinations unknown to me.

The verse of contrition I was given to chant so many years ago has had consequences of its own. It has carried me beyond a simple "I'm sorry" to an appreciation of the circumstances in which we all live, the ways in which we try and fail, and try and fail again. I'm a partner now in the brotherhood and sisterhood of inevitable error and recovery.

Our human lives are "ten thousand beautiful mistakes" as the old masters liked to point out. If my mistakes, willful or unintended, have cost anyone the price of pain or distress, I'm truly sorry. I would like to be free of wrongdoing, but I've found that impossible in life as I know it. Yet I take consolation in acknowledging the mistakes I've made, saying to the world, "This is what I've done. And this is what I am, no better and no worse than you see me now. I trust that you will grant me that much and allow me to go along with it."

Getting What You Want

I N HIS TEACHING of the First Noble Truth, the Buddha asks, "What now is the Noble Truth of suffering?" Answering his own question he goes on to cite the forms that human suffering takes, naming such things as sickness, old age, and death along with the sorrow, pain, grief, and despair that accompany human decay and loss. "Not getting what you want," the Buddha says, "is suffering." What he doesn't say at the time is that *getting* what you want is also suffering.

Wanting is generally thought of as wanting something in particular, a specific object or outcome, like wanting a new car or a bigger house, a different job or mate or hair color or personality. Some "wanters" think bigger than others, wanting an entirely different life from the one they're currently living. Their dissatisfactions are comprehensive and they yearn for a life with more freedom, interest, excitement, adventure, respect, or fame than they're accustomed to getting. But while wanters always want something specific, I've observed that wanting itself is more a state of mind than it is an attraction to a discrete object. A person with a "wanting mind" is perpetually on the lookout for something to want. It's a habit of preferring almost anything other than what one already has, a chronic dissatisfaction with one's circumstance, a persistently distressed mood. A wanting mind is a mind with a predilection toward need.

If wanting is your thing, then it's easy to see how getting what you want won't relieve the suffering of *not* getting what you want. Let's say that you want to write a novel, not just any novel but a really good novel. You tell yourself that if you could just do that, you'd be satisfied. Suppose then you get what you want. You write just the very novel you had in mind. But since wanting is of your very nature, your satisfaction in having written the novel you'd so desired will be short lived, and your wanting will simply transfer itself to a new object of desire. There's no satisfaction in having written a novel unless it gets published. And then of course it must get good reviews and sell well. In such a frame of mind, getting what you want invariably hands you the legacy of an additional want. And so in the end you find yourself dissatisfied with anything less than a national bestseller and a Nobel Prize in literature. And perhaps even that won't satisfy when your success is marred by discovering that you have to share the prize with some poet of whom you'd never even heard. The obvious point here is that wanting and dissatisfaction go hand in hand. And they go hand in hand because wanting is an expression of dissatisfaction. It's not the lack of the thing wanted but the wanting itself that constitutes the suffering.

Buddhists will readily identify the wanting mind with the metaphor of the hungry ghost who can never satisfy its hungers because hunger is of its very nature. Without its hungers, the hungry ghost would cease to exist. The hungry ghost clings to the object of its desire for the sake of identity. Indeed, its desire for the object *is* its identity. This confusing of one's self with the object of one's desire is a huge mistake we humans make, but a common enough mistake at that. What the hungry ghost fears is the loss of itself, and that fear is the source of all its variant clinging.

I LATELY VIEWED A 1987 MOVIE called *Moonstruck* in which Cher, playing Loretta Castorini in the starring role, was still a very young actress. Olympia Dukakis, playing the role of Rose, Loretta's mother, was portrayed as a woman in her mid-sixties with a husband of the same approximate age who had taken a younger woman for a mistress. What Rose wanted to know was what exactly drove her husband toward this behavior. Twice in the movie, she asked other men, "Why do men chase after women?" On the second such occasion, she got an answer that struck her as the truth. "We're afraid we'll die," she was told. One can very well take this as reference to a metaphorical demise, and it certainly would be if, say, my identity was postulated on my attractiveness and sexual desirability in the eyes of younger women. Deprived of any confirmation of that fact, the whole hopeful "person" I cling to as myself would necessarily die away in the face of contrary evidence.

"Look. Chasing after women is about sex. It's a natural appetite," some would say. The viewpoint would seem plausible enough, but my observations leave me unconvinced that it's necessarily that simple. It seems just as likely to me that what individuals are really after in the affairs they pursue is the romance of the affair and not its sex per se. Returning to *Moonstruck*, the husband and mistress were never shown in sexual involvement at all, but at candle-lit tables in intimate restaurants or dressed together for a night at the opera. Among men I've known personally, I've never witnessed a liaison with a younger women that did not involve the effort to recapture the romance they associated with their own lost youth.

But the demise of self-image alone doesn't account for the great lengths people go to in order to keep these flattering fictions viable. Within all such losses lies the premonition of death itself. It's our mortality that drives us toward these hopeless and pathetic delusions. The hunger of the hungry ghost is driven by the fear of death—"If I can earn more, eat more, buy more, run more marathons, get more sex, achieve more fame, maybe I can stave off just a little while longer the certain knowledge that I'm going to die."

When my brother, Rowland, turned fifty, some friends of his were kidding him about getting old. "What's it like to hit the half-century mark?" they wanted to know. My brother's wife was a year older than he, and his response was that he didn't mind being fifty himself but the fact that he was sleeping with a fifty-one-year-old woman took some getting used to. He meant it in jest, but I heard in my brother's joking laughter that there was something of a truth for him in what he'd said. He'd always been sensitive about aging, and perhaps watching his wife age year after year made his own aging reflection in the mirror all the more apparent to him. Later, when a rare and fatal disease overtook him and his death was imminent, I asked him how it was going. "Well, I'm not dying!" was his emphatic response in perfect denial of obvious fact. And among the last exchanges he had with members of the family was to order them out of his hospital room so that he could get some "rest."

Even if you're not a person who's particularly prone to wanting more than life has given, there's still another subtle way in which getting what you want brings suffering. Suppose you want the love of a man or woman whom you've met. You think of this person day and night and sometimes dream of spending your lives together. And then you get what you want and you're finally together with your loved one and have no inclination to want more or other than what you already have in hand. But even then, in the midst of your fresh delight and fulfillment, the possibility of losing the loved one through death or estrangement may very likely weave its subtle distress into your newfound happiness. It's a distress that's inevitable when you consider that nothing lasts. Sooner or later, whatever I have will be taken from me.

It's my observation that it's best to be mindful of what you ask for because you might just get it. But when it comes to persons or things that I genuinely love for their own sakes and not as an extension of my own sense of worth, I say go for it and be willing to pay the price of heartache if you happen to lose what you love. I've never required myself, nor suggested it to anyone else, to live a life of never wanting anything. I love my wife, Karen, and would be heartbroken if she were somehow lost to me. And the same can be said of certain places and things that I've come to love—the fall gathering of crows in the Chico cemetery, the shaded pool on Chico Creek where I swim in the heat of summer, a cup and saucer my daughter gave me, and even an old sharpening stone that once belonged to my mother-in-law, Eloise. I love such things and don't try to temper the strength of my affection in any way.

Love is the very heartbeat of humanity, and if it comes at a cost then so be it—I'll pay my dues when the time comes. I may suffer some, but I'll not suffer from the anxiety of lost possession, because I don't fancy that I own people and things. And I don't consider playing it safe so as to avoid loss and disappointment a good option, because to do so forfeits most of the reason for having any life at all. So I don't ask of myself that I not want to keep at hand the people and things I care most about. What I do ask is that I not complain of the cost of doing so and take my chances along with the rest of humankind, holding in reserve a certain willingness to relinquish what I care most about when the time has come to let go. It's a constant training of the most practical sort, in which I bow to circumstance and set aside, or at the very least put in perspective, whatever troubled yearnings arise to have things go my way.

This willingness to loosen my grip on whatever I'm holding on to is crucial to my wellbeing because circumstances will eventually pry my hand loose regardless. My insistence on clinging to what I want can only make of my life a tense and distressful exercise in "getting," "having," and "holding." Zen Master Yun-men may have had something like this outcome in mind when he said, "I'd rather have nothing than something good." Perhaps he understood how unwilling human nature can be to allow whatever we've gotten hold of to slip once again from our grasp. Yun-men understood that getting what you want is suffering as well.

I don't know about others, but I've never learned how to not want what, in fact, I want. And some of the things I want I'm likely to get. The trick of getting what I want and not unduly suffering as a consequence is the willingness to pass it on. That way I'm a kind of conduit, a "flow-through," an agent of transmission. Something good comes my way and I get to enjoy its brief or, for that matter, long passage through my life on its way to some other destination. It may not be exactly a case of "easy come, easy go." It may, in fact, be hard in the coming and hurt in the going. But it won't hurt nearly so much as trying to stop it in its flow.

In December of 2000, I retook the Buddhist precepts under the direction of a Rinzai Zen Master who gave me the fortunate Dharma name of *Chuan Liu* or "River Willow" in English. I say it was fortunate because while a river willow is a rather small, scrubby, unimpressive tree, it's nonetheless adaptable and good at reseeding the eroding and shifting banks of streams. My teacher gave me a poem to go with the name, picturing the river willow overhanging the moving waters. He wrote:

> Through the long day
> The willow gives its green shade,
> Shelter, water, a soft breeze
> Light dappling the undersurface of the boughs.
> Whatever is given is passed on.

I have lived where river willows secure the banks of mountain streams. I've watched the waters slip under the shady patches their limbs cast upon the current. And I've learned from them how to content myself with whatever soil holds my roots in place, receiving what the river brings and passing it on once more.

Kindness

ROM MY VIEWPOINT, Buddhism is not about getting enlightened—it's about being kind. If I have a chance at the time of my death to take an accounting of what I've done, I won't be asking how enlightened I've become, I'll be asking how much I've shown kindness to others.

This is how the Buddha began, who set out walking the earth not in quest of enlightenment but in search of a means to end the suffering he saw all about him. If I ever hope to realize a generous, loving, merciful, nonviolent human society, I too must carry on the daily practice of generosity, love, mercy, and nonviolence that the Buddha set in motion. This is the practical and ordinary work of the bodhisattva.

And yet the capacity for kindness is an invariable consequence of enlightenment, for enlightenment and compassion are not merely mutually reinforcing but one and the same, two movements of one understanding. And that understanding is the direct knowing that nowhere does there exist a single separate self. The perception of no self *is* one of compassion, since compassion is not so much a matter of feeling as one of identification. If you and I, in all our obvious uniqueness, are yet manifestations of one life and one mind, then what happens to you involves me. I have nothing solely of my own to grasp or defend. Our lives here on earth are grafted on to each other. We share a single root.

However, kindness is something you *do* as much as something you *are*, and while enlightenment teaches you who you are—or more accurately who you *aren't*—it doesn't necessarily tell you what to do with the discovery. What enlightenment does is expose prior limits, as if you'd been a stable-bred foal and had spent the whole of your life in the confinement of a stall, being tossed a daily flake of baled alfalfa and a quarter bucket of oats for your feed. Then one day the whole face of the barn falls off and you and all your stable mates go whinnying into the sudden fields, exposed to immensely more space and options than any had ever dreamed existed. And while the green growing fields without walls stretch out to the far horizon with nothing to restrain you from galloping until your lungs burst, you'll still have to learn simple things like which of the wild plants to feed on and where to bed down at night. Enlightenment is a beginning, but not an end. And it doesn't come with a set of specific instructions. It takes practice to learn to run with the rest of herd.

Old habits of mind and body will outlast the force of the deepest enlightenment. I may very well see through the delusion of a separate self and still go on acting in its behalf, defending a ghost of myself that never existed. The cultivation of compassion is largely a matter of stopping what I've been doing. If I want to do kindness, I must stop doing unkindness. If I want to do generosity, I must stop doing greed. If I want to do love, I must stop doing hate.

This is a simple fact, a formulation of consequence: what we do is what we get. Or as Martin Luther King Jr. put it, "The ends are pre-existent in the means." Or again, as Zen Master Dogen insisted, "Training and enlightenment are one and the same." It may be a tautotology to assert that until we stop doing what we're doing we're still doing what we're doing, but if the transparent logic of this goes unacknowledged, I might very well find myself in pursuit of enlightenment without having undertaken to free myself from habits of self-interest and greed.

I don't ask of anyone—including myself—that they be occupying any level whatsoever of enlightenment. I only ask that we live kindly and decently, with care and concern for all the beings of the world. I don't have to possess a superior insight or any insight other than that of the ordinary mind in order to work for the cessation of suffering. To experience a mind-shattering awakening might be a marvelous experience, like nothing else any of us will ever know, but it's useless if it doesn't move the hand that reaches out to heal the world's ills.

Willa Cather has written, "When kindness has left people, even for a few moments, we become afraid of them, as if their reason had left them." Kindness, you see, is our natural condition. If we abandon kindness in favor of the pursuit of personal enlightenment, we risk fearing our own faces for dread of what we see there.

The Feast

SOMETIMES when I think things are going my way, they aren't. And when I fail to notice this it's usually because I'm not paying sufficient attention. It's much better to keep watch over events as they unfold than to form doubtful impressions of them. That way I'm given a chance to notice that things aren't necessarily the way I think they are. The fact is that life refuses to be shaped into conformity with my own hopeful version of events. There's humility, gentleness, even wisdom that comes with the discovery of personal limits. I know all this, and yet I sometimes forget that my happy imaginings exercise no influence over the way events actually unfold. That's when I'm most likely to think I have things under control, failing to notice indications that suggest otherwise.

FOR TWO YEARS NOW, I've served as Senior Buddhist Chaplain at High Desert State Prison, a maximum-security prison in Susanville, California. The Buddhist inmates at the prison had been without a teacher for more than four years at the time, and so

I was asked if I would please come. I had my plans pretty well mapped out at the time and didn't really want to undertake another responsibility. Furthermore, High Desert State Prison is on the east side of the Sierra Nevada Range, a two-and-a-half-hour drive from the west side town of Chico where I live. I said I'd think it over.

The decision was taken out of my hands the day I first laid eyes on the prison complex and met the first of my potential students, most of whom are serving life sentences. After passing through the outer perimeter of the prison with its lethal web of electrically charged wiring and after negotiating a seemingly endless series of electronically controlled gates that opened and shut behind me, I finally arrived on a catwalk outside cell C5—218 where I peered through a thin slit of a window at the face of a nineteen-year-old Asian boy who was serving a sentence for first-degree murder and wouldn't even be considered for parole until he was in his mid-fifties. I told him who I was and what I'd come for. At first he seemed confused by the information, wondering what my appearance at his cell meant for him. But then, he suddenly brightened, a smile breaking out on his face, and he asked, "Are you my teacher?" And without a thought for the consequences, I said, "Yes, I'm your teacher." "Are we going to have Buddhist services?" "We'll have services," I told him. And so for all my plans to the contrary, life had turned me in a direction, the difficulties and blessings of which I could never have foretold.

The first Buddhist service in the C-Yard complex brought me sixty inmates, the guards patting them down one after another as they filed into the chapel to remove their shoes and hats and find themselves a cushion or chair to sit on. If circumstances were strange and unfamiliar to me, it was equally so for the inmates, most of whom were Southeast Asians familiar with Theravada and Pure Land Buddhist traditions but unacquainted with Zen. Whatever their expectation was for a teacher, I wasn't it. For one thing, I'm Scandinavian, not Thai, Burmese, or Vietnamese. For another I wasn't a Theravada or Pure Land priest. I'm a Zen teacher, and when my own teachers put me to the task of teaching, it was understood that my qualifications were to teach in the Zen tradition in which I was trained. I explained this to the inmates, telling them that I would offer them what I could but that I wasn't authorized to teach in other traditions. I assured them that while Zen services might seem unfamiliar to them at first, they would be less so in time. "The elements of Buddhist practice that I'll teach you will be those that are central to all Buddhist traditions," I explained. At the time, that seemed right and reasonable to me.

But "right" and "reasonable" or not, it wasn't going to work. For a year and a half, things went seemingly well. The inmates arrived faithfully for meeting after meeting and did whatever was asked of them. It seemed to me that High Desert Zen Sangha was a reality, and that together we were finding the Way.

It was a period in which I had the unfortunate comfort of reading only those positive evidences that left me feeling no need to adjust what I was doing. Still, from the very beginning, some of the inmates had repeatedly lobbied for a ceremonial feast, dedicated to Amitabha Buddha of the Pure Land, at which they could celebrate the Pure Land and give thanks to the ancestors. I kept putting the request aside, repeating that I was a Zen teacher and could only offer what I knew. And then one day I drove over the mountains to conduct a Zen service to which no one came. I laid out the thirty zafus donated by Chico residents, placing them in five rows of six each. I set up the altar with an Avalokiteshvara statue and another of the Buddha. I lit a candle and readied the incense for zazen. And when the time came for my students to appear, the guards told me they had refused to leave their cells. When this was repeated a second time, I sat in the painful silence of the chapel and looked long and hard at the empty rows of cushions.

I don't know if I can really say that I'd said or done anything wrong but it hadn't helped much to be "right." Right or wrong, I'd been effectively shut down. My reading of circumstances had been partial, failing to register anything contrary to my optimistic view of things. But regardless of how well I thought things were going and regardless of how reasonable and justified my actions had been, the work of eighteen months to build a sangha at High Desert State Prison had been brought to a halt. One of the older inmates who'd led the request for an Amitabha feast had called for a boycott, and once again C-Yard was without a Buddhist teacher. I'd lost control of the situation, or to put it more accurately, I'd lost the illusion of control.

Nonetheless, not getting my own way has often been a blessing in my life, and this turned out to be no exception. All the stiffness about being right and principled went out of me, and alternatives were clarified. I could either walk away from the whole painful and awkward situation, telling myself that I'd done my best and leaving High Desert State Prison for good. Or I could negotiate with the inmates. In the end, I couldn't walk away. I'd come to love my students and couldn't imagine leaving them if it was possible to stay.

I was brought by "misfortune" to listen this time, *forced* to listen actually, to what my students had been saying about a feast, because I obviously hadn't understood the importance of it to them. I'd watched them come to the chapel, service after service, faithfully doing Zen practice under my direction, and had somehow failed to see that we were heading toward a breakup. When I finally talked to the elder inmate who'd shut me down, what I learned from him humbled me and brought me closer to the view of the world held by my students. "When you came, we thought you'd be on our side," he said. "If you would just meet us halfway. . ." he went on. "We have no joy here in prison. A feast would be a celebration. We could have some fun. I've been here twenty years, but the younger ones need this even more than I do, though they may not know it yet."

He sat across from me in the "common" area at a little metal table bolted to the floor, the metal stools we sat on bolted down as well. He was dressed in the prison issue of worn and faded blue pants and shirt, indistinguishable from the clothing of any other inmate. Beyond him were the tiers of cells, one of which had been his only home for half his life and where he might very well end whatever years life would allot him. And while we talked, an armed guard stood over us to prevent physical contact. He had virtually no control over the details of his outer life, the activities of every hour of the twenty years he'd spent in prison dictated by others. The only reason he was sitting talking to me now was because I'd requested it. Yet, ironically, he could at a word bring the students back to services or extend the boycott as he saw fit. Before we parted, he asked, "So, what can I tell them?" "Tell them we'll have a feast," I said.

I SOMETIMES FORGET not to trust my own reading of surface appearances. I allow essential doubt to languish. I lull myself into a sort of lazy and comforting perception of circumstances and so lose touch with fact. When I do so, it's a lapse of the first and last principle of Zen: pay attention. And a sangha? I thought that my students at High Desert State Prison were so set upon with demeaning and demoralizing conditions that I, as their teacher, was called upon to create for them a refuge in which they could find at least a few moments respite from their ordinary deprivations. I characterized them as helpless, and myself as the helper. I underestimated their strength and didn't take them into equal partnership in the forming of our sangha. I didn't remember that I needed them every bit as much as they might need me. They taught me that and helped me return to the roots of my practice.

What I've learned from not getting my way at High Desert State Prison is that believing I'm in control of a situation is an isolating perception that leads to certain error. I thought I was "in charge" of Buddhist practice at the prison, falsely depending on that fact for maintaining control of a situation that by its very nature is always threatening to go to pieces. But I wasn't in charge. What little control I'd managed to exert was only by the grace and consent of my students. And isn't this the way it always is? Isn't actual circumstance the final arbiter of what is or isn't going to happen? Has it ever really been within anyone's power to dictate outcomes? At their insistence, the students and I are meeting each other halfway now. I'm on their side and they're on mine.

They dutifully practice daily zazen, and I'm learning the Pure Land chant that calls upon Amitabha.

Sangha

S ANGHA IS A SANSKRIT WORD that in its narrowest sense has as its referent the community of those who follow the Buddha's teaching. As limited as this application of the term might be, the community of Buddhist followers nonetheless consists of a vast network of sangha within sangha arranged like concentric rings of mutual inclusion. The Chico Zen Sangha, for example, which I once founded and teach is a sangha in its own right. But it is as well a sangha within the larger sangha of both Soto and Rinzai Zen, having established formal affiliation with both traditions. But the Zen tradition itself is in turn a sangha within the larger sangha of the whole Buddhist community. Whether it be Tibetan, Theravada, Insight Meditation, Pure Land, or whatever, the community of those who follow the Buddha's teaching constitutes one vast worldwide sangha.

But it doesn't end there, for it is taught that Buddha nature pervades the whole universe, a concept descriptive of a virtually limitless sangha comprised of the intimate and intricate interweaving of all beings into one seamless whole. This being so, what is there to exclude? What stone, what drifting feather, what clot of earth or sky, what soiled and drunken soul sleeping in the doorway of the convenience store, what cranky or cheerful clerk at the checkout stand, what mother, father, child, what family rich or poor, hungry or full, what being of any sort, anywhere, at any time, is *not* sangha?

A sangha category inclusive of everything *is* everything and isn't a category at all, Buddhist or otherwise. Ironically, the notion of a fellowship of all beings might seem so vast as to seem somehow remote from whatever beings lie readily at hand, more of a disembodied thought than an expression of immediate reality. A sangha inclusive of all beings is a thought difficult to wrap the mind around, a little like trying to relate the infinite scope of the universe to the bit of ground you happen to be standing on. And yet, while a sangha comprised of Buddhist followers holds for me a particular sense of belonging, the most intimate instances of Dharma fellowship have sprung up from within this greater sangha in places and among people I could never have anticipated. Sangha, after all, implies something other than the simple existence of contiguous beings, no matter how radically integrated and interdependent they might be. At the very least, it implies the *perception* of such interdependence. Sangha is a realized relationship between beings acknowledged by the participating parties, and this participation consists of more than merely identifying with others, and is primarily a matter of doing something with others. When sangha happens, it happens as a living event, often unforeseen and unattached to any formal tradition.

I CAME UPON SUCH AN EVENT in late March of 1986 in a barren dirt lot adjacent to the town dump in Barstow, California. It was there on the windswept high desert amidst the drifting dust and flies and burning trash of the dump that the Great Peace March for Global Nuclear Disarmament had set up camp on its 3700-mile, 225-day walk from Los Angeles to Washington DC. When Karen and I, on our way east to Shoshone at the southern entrance to Death Valley, chanced upon the Barstow camp, the marchers had just received word that their sponsoring organization, PRO-Peace, had dissolved and no longer existed. Along with the collapse of PRO-Peace, the marchers had lost their main source of funding, most of their equipment and supplies, and all of the logistical support they'd counted on during the long walk east. With this bad news, the camp was breaking up and many participants were heading back home. But not all were.

Some were sticking it out, seeing what might be done to keep the march alive. As busloads of walkers departed and tents were torn down, the remaining tents were gathered together to form a temporary community out of those who remained. It was a hard time and a decisive moment for many, families sometimes splitting up as some stayed and others headed back home. A college-age daughter, seeing her father off at the Greyhound bus depot, headed back to the camp where the women were heating water to wash the dirt out of each other's hair.

When the exodus homeward had ended, 600 remained in the Barstow camp. What Karen and I saw the day we arrived there was the birth of a sangha, an *ad hoc* sangha responsive to the need of the moment, made up of members without formal lineage or credentials of any kind other than those of a human being. It was a sangha of the best kind with a consummate aim to realize a merciful and compassionate outcome and to do so by virtue of a willing cooperation with each other. Within hours, the camp had set up a kitchen tent and identified those among them with experience in cooking. They'd set up a first-aid station and found members with nursing or doctoring capabilities. They'd also implemented a governing structure in which all 600 members could participate directly in decisions. They'd given themselves the name of "Peace City," and had drafted a statement of purpose with the following preamble:

> The Great Peace March for Global Nuclear Disarmament is an abolitionist movement. We believe that great social change comes about when the will of the people becomes focused on a moral imperative. By marching for nine months across the United States, we will create a non-violent focus for positive change; the imperative being that nuclear weapons are politically, socially, economically, and morally unjustifiable, and that, in any number, they are unacceptable. It is the responsibility of a democratic government to implement the will of its people, and it is the will of the people of the United States and many other nations to end the nuclear arms race.

This preamble was written and approved on the spot by people most of whom had never before known one another. Nonetheless, on that dirt lot in Barstow, California, 600 marchers, by their own courage, trust, and good will, had undertaken a task deemed certain to fail, and had bound themselves to the performance of the most difficult of the four bodhisattva vows: "Beings are numberless; I vow to enlighten them all." The undaunted heart of the Great Peace March Sangha had given birth right there in the Barstow dump to a movement that brought the hearts of a nation to their support. While they sometimes had little to eat and no adequate shelter, they persevered, fed by their sense of the right and the good and sheltered by courage to continue on. Despite predictions of failure, their ranks gradually swelled to 1200 marchers and they were met in town after town with well-wishers who aided them along the way.

One might say that it was love that at last delivered the Great Peace March Sangha to the very steps of the Capitol in Washington DC where they were met by 15,000 supporters.

SANGHA IS A HEART OF INCLUSION. It's the act of turning toward rather than away from each other.

For me, sangha is not constrained by definition or sectarian affiliation. Sangha is where you find it. Jesus is quoted as saying, "Wherever two or more are gathered in my name, there am I." I would say as well, "Wherever two or more are gathered in the name of kindness and healing, there is sangha." And it's found everywhere if you think to look for it, springing up in response to circumstance. Sangha isn't necessarily borne of extremity either and can occur virtually without notice, not being perceived by anyone including its participants as being anything out of the ordinary. Members of the high school girls' choir washing cars on a Saturday morning to pay their way to the regional finals might well be such a sangha; or the folks in their work boots and gloves gathered at dawn in the city parking lot for the day's creek and park cleanup; or the women sitting round a table stitching a quilt for auction at the Center for Nonviolence; or the volunteers spooning out soup for the homeless at the Jesus Center.

In my mind, I draw a parallel between the great Soto teacher Dogen's observation that "the koan appears naturally in daily life," and my own lifetime observation that sangha as well appears naturally in daily life. The incidental formation of a naturally arising sangha gives testimony to the living sangha itself, arising of its own volition just as it once did in the time of the historical Buddha.

I'm glad to take refuge in a traditional Zen sangha that traces its roots to the teachings handed down to it by its Soto and Rinzai ancestors. But I also realize that sangha is not so much a matter of form or lineage as it is a gathering of the moment. Sangha is a state of mind, a capacity of the heart. In this sense, Buddhism has no monopoly on sangha. At this very moment, some little band of people gathered at a public event or a neighbor's house or a downtown street corner may very well be plotting to do some good in the world, something borne of kindness that's suited to a particular need. It is this unlikely and unforeseen sangha of the human heart that I most take refuge in.

The Cross of the Moment

We would rather be ruined than changed.
We would rather die in our dread
than climb the cross of the moment
and let our illusions die.
        —W. H. AUDEN

WE'D DO WELL to heed these words of Auden's, for we live in a time in which the truth of the matter is sometimes too dreadful to admit. How is it that our species with its inherent capacity for kindness and with its eye for beauty has come to the place where we turn against each other with devastating instruments of warfare and lay waste to the land itself in a misguided quest for wealth? Would we really rather be ruined than changed? Are we so caught up in present schemes of fear and ambition that we'd rather die than acknowledge the dreadful consequence of perpetuating such schemes? In an age where warfare divides the world into hostile encampments and global warming threatens the balance and survival of planetary life, Auden's words are not hyperbole. We must awaken now, as I know we can would we but suffer our time on the cross.

Awakening begins with acknowledging the true fact of a matter, no better and no worse than it is. Could we but let our illusions die, then our bodies, yours and mine, and our greater body, which is that of the earth itself, might yet find a way to survive. It is told that the young Siddhartha was born to privileged circumstance, living a youthful life insulated from the realities of others. But when he saw the hardships suffered beyond the protective barrier of the castle walls, he found his own favored circumstances intolerable to bear. The birth of that conscience was the first and greatest of the Buddha's awakenings. He climbed the cross of the moment, leaving all his prior illusions of privilege and separateness to die. Preferring even the most radical change to a life of moral ruin, he embraced the misfortunes of common humanity to see what might be done to make things better.

Nothing matters more than that this young prince tried. Had he hoped to avert humankind from the chronic self-induced suffering of its own ambitions, he failed. Twenty-six hundred years later, with the power of energy harnessed to our pursuits, we have carried greed to a length and breadth and momentum the Buddha could not have imagined. For those of us who see this, we can only do as the Buddha once did, and try as best we can to make things better, to make our lives worthy of the gift of a human body and mind. Our species is capable of averting the disaster toward which we are heading if only we can find the will to do so. And if we fare no better now than the Buddha did in the time of his trying, then we do well to cultivate our best bedside manner, for we will be witnessing the demise of the best and worst of what we call civilization. And if it comes to that, we must be ready to hold the dying hand of humankind, giving whatever comfort is left in us to give, and doing so until the last of us has drawn breath.

But it needn't come to that. I refuse to succumb to grief and I do not call for despair. I call for sorrow perhaps and a little tenderness and forgiveness for all the illusions we have cultivated in our collective denial. But I don't call for cynicism or defeat. All who follow the Buddha Way have vowed to take on the impossibility of saving all beings, and it's time to act on that vow. It is told that long ago a young god threw his dying weight upon a cross and moved all heaven and earth alone. Any one of us, at any moment, can do as much. We can dare to look beyond the comforting tales we tell ourselves, and we can undertake whatever radical change of heart and mind and action is needed to salvage what's good about us. Whenever even one soul out of the many millions of humankind wills herself or himself to take just this first step toward sanity and kindness, then, in that very act, salvation is enacted and all is *not* ruined and beauty breathes once more in our midst.

Desert Places

They cannot scare me with their empty spaces
Between stars—on stars where no human race is.
I have it in me so much nearer home
To scare myself with my own desert places.
    —ROBERT FROST

PERHAPS WE HUMANS NEED FIRST to get lost in order to discover where we are. I sometimes get lost in my own kitchen or seated at a desk where I've worked for years or even while looking into a face as familiar as my own reflection in the bathroom mirror. Getting lost is a way of opting out of the arbitrary familiarity we impose on ourselves for the sake of a falsely comforting reassurance that things are as we imagine them to be and that we are who we think we are. And getting lost can come upon you unexpectedly and with a force that shakes loose all prior certainties.

I've done enough wilderness hiking and backpacking in my life to literally lose my way more than once. And when it dawns on me that I don't know where I am, there's always that sudden intake of the breath, the pulse racing a bit, the mind tightening, a little fear tripping along the nerves. I think loss of place for me is often accompanied with a certain frightening sense of loss of self. It's as if, having stepped out of any location known to me, I've somehow stepped out of my own skin as well. I don't quite know what to make of myself in a territory that's unanticipated and thus markedly foreign. For just that moment before I get out the topographical map and start relocating myself, I get a chance to start all over and figure out anew who I am. All in all, getting lost is an opportunity to acquaint myself with myself.

I'M SEVENTY-FIVE YEARS OLD as I write this. I was forty-three when I went into the desert. The central California college where I taught had adopted a schedule that left me free for the month of January. I wanted to take a walking trip but the mountains were snowed in, so I decided to try the desert. Twenty miles north of Yuma on the California shore of the Colorado River is a small camp called Picacho. From Picacho to Walter's Camp sixty miles upstream, the river flows through a desert wilderness. Here I could find the isolation I wanted, and the Colorado River would serve as a lifeline. I sent to Denver for topographical maps.

When the parcel arrived from the U.S. Geological Survey and I had flattened the maps on the table and the first flush of enthusiasm had subsided, I began to see more clearly the venture I was undertaking. California's low desert has few distinguishing characteristics and so the contour lines on the maps appeared as a visual labyrinth of uncertain character, twisted so randomly over such vast areas that they presented no discernible pattern at all. I was brought back to my first journey through the lens of a microscope, focusing through and beyond the sentient surface of things until a new order of being materialized out of the old. I was coming to understand that the organization I discovered under the microscope was the organization of my very own being as well. I saw for the first time where all substance spilled over into the substance of absolutely all the rest. Even the most familiar forms—a leaf, a stem, a patch of my own skin—were penetrated to a level of organization where all unique and distinguishing characteristics dissolve into an alien simplicity.

On map, the formless desert called up once more the unnerving probability that all our human order is arbitrary—that our mode of perception is but a faith, a tenuous reprieve from absorption into an imminent, incalculable universal wilderness. In the end, probably to accommodate my own apprehensions, I devised a simple, even symmetrical itinerary. I would drive to Picacho and hike up the river for forty miles where the topographical showed a single isolated dot labeled the "Draper Cabin." At that point I would float my pack across the river and hike back down the Arizona side.

At Picacho, the river was not at all what I'd expected. It was heavy and dark and swifter than I'd thought it would be—a sullen river. Having none of the lightness of mountain rivers I'd known, the Colorado was a dull viscous flood that scraped and sucked the spongy clay that lined its banks. One could not reach the river without sinking to the ankles in mud. I looked up Ken Simmons at the ranger facility, gave him my itinerary, found out the rattlers were dormant, and that I'd be on my own about as soon as I'd walked out of earshot.

Simmons was right—one had committed himself to his own care the minute he'd set the first ridge between himself and the camp. It was as if I'd dropped myself into a cunning maze of no design at all. If anything went wrong in such a place, I'd have scant chance of being found. In moving up river, I discovered I couldn't follow the shoreline at all because the river was flanked by swampy, impenetrable thickets. I'd work up brushy gullies only to find myself pocketed within vertical faces. I'd pick my way along a shale ridge until it turned back on itself, forcing me in a circle as if on the eroded rim of an exhausted volcano, or until the ridge terminated, leaving me stranded on some steep, crumbling bluff. And when I tried to work my way back into the flat near the river, I was prevented by the shore growth. By the time I'd lost the light, I'd penetrated no nearer the river than the tip of some alkaline lagoon where I sat at the lagoon's edge on a crusty mosaic of contracted clay left by the receding water and tried to put together a supper.

Then something wonderful happened. The moon rose over Arizona, yellow and full. When the moon had cleared the horizon, a coyote lifted a wail into the night sky. And then others, not only across the river flat but in the desert hills to the west of me. And nearby, somewhere in the thicket, the wheezing bray of burros. These too were answered from the hills and from across the river. On all sides, an affirmation of flesh and spirit that seemed for the instant to master all that blank desert space. On my patch of cracked clay, I would have thrown my voice in with the others but that the merest embarrassed hesitation turned my will inward, and in an instant of regretful self-denial, I struck off the sound in my own throat. Save for the solitary hiss of the camp stove, the desert reverted to silence. Later, before bedding down, I called out into the desert night with a voice I didn't at once recognize as my own.

In the following days, the travel went better, but as the hours and miles from Picacho grew greater so did my sense of isolation. The crumbling ridges rose under my feet one after another, heaps of rock-trash to be surmounted. From the vantage of any height, I could survey a waste of such ridges radiating 360 degrees around me, a great disc of wounded earth spread out to the limits of sight. In all that space, I seemed to be the only sentient creature to bear witness to the moment. I walked out my days on a stranded planet ringed by a sundering horizon.

On the fifth day, the wind blew. It swept in from the northeast, a sharp January wind that filled the air with dust and rattled the mesquite where it clung to the exposed flat. The afternoon found me isolated on a great plain where the visibility was so poor I couldn't maintain direction without a compass. The winter sun leaked through from the south and stretched a dull shadow out before me on the crusty sand so that I was hurrying forward into my own shade. Then, at the very margin where the reflecting surface slipped under my advancing shadow, the merest suggestion of pattern flickered into relief, something too symmetrical to have been there, and then lost to sight again because the lowering winter sun washed out everything like an over-exposed negative. But then I caught it again—the faintest linear depression, like that of tire track, so weathered it was barely discernible. But definite enough if one positioned it at just the right slant to the sun. And finally two parallel tracks bisecting the desert plain east and west.

However unlikely it seemed, some wheeled vehicle had made its way across the desert and apparently gone down to the river. I would not have thought that one could penetrate to the river from this plain, but following the tracks as best I could in the failing light, I found where they wound through some open patches in the shore growth and emerged on the bank of the river. Where a finger of rock jutted into the current, forming a sluggish backwash on the upstream side, stood an old, square-cab truck with a high flat windshield and narrow spoke wheels. The truck was an oxidized green, and mounted on its bed was an aluminum camper with a door in the rear and a window on either side. A line had been strung from the camper to a metal pole wedged somehow into the rocks, and from this line hung three or four chalky white T-shirts and a pair of khaki pants. Even in my astonishment at finding a camp there, I thought to consider how anyone in these circumstances could have gotten those T-shirts so white.

When I had come to within a few yards, a face suddenly showed in one of the windows and as quickly disappeared. In an instant the camper door opened, and the face from the window took me in for a long moment and then said quite matter-of-factly, "It's a cold wind. Would you like to step in for a tin of coffee?" So we sat in his tiny camper and drank strong coffee from tin cups. His name was Hank Evert. He was a short, thin man, about my size and age. He wore clean khakis, a T-shirt as starchy white as those on the line, tennis shoes, and a baseball cap. His hair was cut short, the ends looking chopped the way a man's hair does when he must use a mirror and scissors to cut his own. As the tracks in the plain had shown, he had engineered himself a route across the desert, coming in from highway 78 thirty-eight miles to the west. He lived on that very spot twelve months of the year, going out to Yuma for supplies only when he could no longer avoid doing so. I asked him about the Draper cabin. He'd heard of it but had never seen it. "Nothing up there," as far as he knew.

That night I made camp within sight of that antique truck where it rested on the river shore like some beached ship whose bewildered crew had long ago wandered off and lost themselves to the desert. I cooked supper in the dark, turning up the hood of my parka against an icy wind that raked the bamboo and yellowed the flame of the pack stove. A candle-lantern flickered in the window of the camper and, from time to time, the shadow of a man shone on the glass. I felt him there, sitting in his T-shirt and sneakers behind the shield of corrugated aluminum, less than forty yards separating the two of us. And for the first time since I'd left Picacho, solitude slid over into loneliness.

Further north the terrain became even more difficult. I was blocked at every point and the greatest effort yielded little progress. It bothered me that I didn't really know where I was. On a previous day, I had come upon a great knob of rock with ridges radiating out from it like points on huge stone star. This formation rose above the general level of the desert, and I thought to climb it and see if I could lay out a better route for myself. But once on the crown, I was astonished to find a survey marker—a round metal tablet fixed permanently in the stone, looking as strange to me in all that desolation as would some artifact from a previous civilization. Engraved on its face were the words, "U.S. Dept. of Interior; Geological Survey; 758 ft."

I dug out of my pack the topographical quadrangle designated "Picacho, S.W.," and my finger, tracing over the brown contours west of the river, came to rest on a tiny dome of concentric rings topped by a triangular symbol and the number 758. So, by authority of an agency of the federal government, I knew for a brief respite exactly where I was. I found this strangely reassuring. But now in the difficult country further north, I'd scramble from sunrise to sunset not knowing if I'd advanced eight miles that day or eighteen. I carried three topographical maps and I no longer had any idea which map I was on.

BY THE MORNING OF THE SEVENTH DAY, this uncertainty had begun to weigh on me. I'd consumed more than half my provisions and, by plan, should have begun my return south to Picacho. As it was, I didn't even know how many hours and miles still lay between me and the Draper cabin. The same morning was all but lost before I forced my passage over a great saw-toothed ridge and it occurred to me to mark the spot in case I couldn't make the river crossing and was forced to come back this way. In the wash below, I found the trunk of a dead yucca, bleached and spongy and light as balsa wood. I carried it onto the ridge, where I gathered loose stones and stacked them around to secure it like a post. I didn't at the time register how illogical it was to suppose that, in an environment where any single acre was indistinguishable from any other, I would chance again upon a solitary post on a ridge. For all practical purposes, I'd been lost since the day I left Picacho, but my nerves were still screwed to a useless survey map and a $6.98 compass.

The yucca post was out of sight before it was out of shouting distance, as I was at once forced onto a bushy flat so overgrown that I was reduced to crawling in the hollows beneath the limbs. I brought myself by this means out into an alkali plain where the sudden light reflecting off the chalky alkali ash stabbed at my eyes. I swallowed some aspirin, washing them down with what little water I had left. Alkali ash spilled over the tops of my socks, and the shuffling scar left in my own wake was the sole spoor to disfigure that whole lifeless expanse. I rested a moment to still the throbbing in my head; and in that pause, the silence shut down on me like the lid of a coffin.

I saw the cabin when it was still a quarter mile distant. It stood, as the map had shown, on a clear rise against the river. The cabin was backed up to a rocky hillock, and at first sight I thought a landslide had buried the rear of the structure. Later I was to learn that Draper had fashioned a shelter that was half burrow and half cabin, the cabin serving as an extension to a cave he had dug into the hillside. I dropped my pack against the frame of the cabin and sat down and leaned back myself. My heart beat in my eyes, and I shut them and held very still. I had hardly glanced at the cabin more than to see that it had a dirt floor, was skinned over with dried mud and twigs, and that the window frames were empty of glass. I was oppressed by the place. What sort of creature would live like this anyway? What on earth had I hoped to find here? I had to think hard to remind myself that I hadn't hoped to find anything, that Draper's cabin was only coincidental with my location for the river crossing. Then why was I nearly sick to tears with loss and aggravation?

I drew a pot of water at the river and carried it up to the cabin and ate a portion of granola and powdered milk. And then, still feeling listless and sick, I quite illogically ate the next day's portion, imagining I suppose that this would make me feel better. My forehead and neck were feverish, and I began to worry that I might be coming down with some real illness. What if I were sick with flu for several days and couldn't travel? I fell asleep at last, propped-up against the cabin, wondering if Draper were ever sick here and how he managed without help.

When I awoke the sun had shifted low on the horizon, leaving me in the shade of the cabin. A chill wind swung the cabin door sluggishly back and forth on rusty hinges. My headache got up with me, so I carried it and my pack down to the river shore where I planned to make camp on a sandy shelf near the water's edge. I was stained with alkali ash, my hair gummy with dirt and congealed sweat. For a while I merely sat and watched where the gray water slid over some rocks. Far over on the Arizona side, a floating clump of soggy brush circled round and round where it was stalled in a backwater against the bluffs. At last I stripped and edged out a little into the quiet water near shore. The cold seemed to run up my bones, and I shivered in the wind. I dipped a washcloth and held it to my forehead. The water leaked into my eyes and stung.

Up on the bank my pack lay tilted against a rock, and further up in the clearing I could catch the outline of Draper's cabin projecting a little beyond the brow of the hill. For reasons that don't at all seem clear now, it occurred to me that I might as well cross the river right then and there and make camp on the Arizona side. I waded back on shore and stuffed my boots and clothes into my pack and cinched it down tight, wrapping it in a heavy plastic bag I'd brought for that purpose. Shivering, I carried the pack into the shallows and floated it out until the water had risen to my waist. The pack rode high, and when I tried my weight on it, I saw that it would make a good raft.

But already I was having misgivings. How far downstream would I be carried before I gained the far shore? Was there any assurance that when I got there, I'd be able to penetrate to dry land? What if I were stranded on some strip of mucky clay and had to reenter the water and float further downstream? How long could I endure the cold? And what if by some freak chance I should lose my pack in the current and have it swept away downstream, leaving me naked on the shore with no provisions whatsoever? I bound myself to the pack by a short length of line. If one of us were lost downstream, it might as well be both. When I'd gotten into the water deep enough that I was losing my footing, I looked out across the slick of water to an Arizona shore blurred with pain, and a voice said, "No." And, for once, I listened.

Dawn was a resurrection, hungry and without pain. The river slid soundlessly between silenced hills. The sun hung suspended in its rising. My morning stove sang in the stillness. When I let myself, I could appreciate how well Draper had built for his needs. He'd set his shelter into the hill so that he was shielded from the northeast wind. He'd given it a frame that hadn't sagged. He'd mortised posts and lintels for the door and window frames. He'd beveled the sills, and he'd laid over it all a sheathing of twigs and mud that one still couldn't see daylight through. Whatever else Draper was, he was also a man much like myself—methodical, precise, a man who took pains to make things right. The cabin asserted the man, its simple intentional geometry held over against all the accidental complexity of the surrounding desert, a signature, saying, "This is who I am." I was helped to better understand the ritual of the campsite—tent set just so, lines snug, down aired and fluffed, the kitchen laid out, stove, fuel flask, pots, water canteen, the pack conveniently positioned. A procedure and design born out of more than merely practical considerations. A reasoned ceremony daily reenacted under peril of a reasonless universe. The mind's stay against being taken in unaware.

That morning at the Draper cabin I was the troubled guest of a man whose thought I hadn't meant to reach. But I lingered too long in the shadows he'd cast about the place, and whatever I found in Draper that reassured, he was yet a fearsome host. How could I reconcile myself to a man who'd carved his shelter like a premature grave into the very earth, who'd submitted to absolute solitude, who'd yielded utterly to the desert, who'd broken with his own kind and come here to live out his hours in self-exile fronting the indifferent hills? I suspect I resisted Draper not because he was alien and inconceivable to me but because he wasn't. After all, I'd come here too. I wasn't so much troubled by Draper's desert places as by my own.

At noon I started my return south. I left hungry, a recompense exacted for the lunch I squandered the day before. Finding a canyon that led away from the river, I chanced it and it paid off in an open plateau that stretched above the river flats for miles. Toward evening the plateau broke up, forcing me once more to scramble and pick my route. I was working down a ridge back toward the river when I saw it—the bleached trunk of the yucca still secured in its base of stones. An impossible chance encounter. The irony was that I couldn't at first recall what the marker was supposed to remind me to do. I had come upon it without need as on a discarded crutch surprised in a closet weeks after the bone has healed. The stones that held the post upright showed raw where I'd unearthed them and clots of dirt still clung to their darker faces. Yet the urgency that had wedged them into place was already something of a stranger to me. I studied the ridge to the south where it rose beyond the intervening wash in a confusion of disintegrating spires. What was I to remember? To go down to the tip of the ridge, circumventing it in the flat near the river? Or was I to take the ridge somewhere further up? It would have been useful to know, but was no longer crucial. In the end I remembered to go up into the rocks where the ridge split and let me through to the country beyond.

THIRTY-TWO YEARS HAVE COME and gone since I walked out of the camp at Picacho and lost myself to the desert. Nothing much has changed in that regard, except that I've gotten used to being lost, always moving through unfamiliar territory to the country beyond. It's an unavoidable human circumstance. We've all of us walked off the map, though we like to imagine otherwise. The human journey out and back recorded here in the details of one man's venture into a desert wilderness is the journey of human consciousness into the desert of the mind.

If you think you are unacquainted with getting lost, know that sooner or later you'll discover your own desert places and then you'll know you're lost. Perhaps it's only those few who have given themselves completely over to the bare reality of their circumstances, like Draper and Hank Evert, who truly know where they are. And of course they know they're lost, but no more lost than you and I. I know for a certainty that every soul ever born on this spinning fragment that we call "Earth" and that is itself but the billionth fraction of an incomprehensible galaxy forever streaming outward into an incalculable expanding universe—is lost. None of us has a hint as to where we are. And we are as alone as anyone who ever set up solitary camp somewhere in the desert we call life.

The Ordinary

*I*F YOU'RE PANNING FOR GOLD, anything else that settles in the pan is just waste to be gotten out of the way. Stones, moss, silt, the nymphs of aquatic flies are just so much debris to be discarded in favor of even the smallest particle of that one rare metal that you've priced above the ordinary.

Zen Master Dogen cautions against preferences that elevate one's tastes above what's commonly at hand. In the *Tenzo Kyokan*, Dogen instructs those who would undertake the practice of chief cook in a Buddhist monastery: "It was once said by a great teacher that priests do not differentiate between various foods just as fire does not differentiate between various sorts of firewood. If we are sincere when cooking, even the coarsest food can help us to exhibit the seed of Buddhahood." Even the coarsest of *anything* can help us to exhibit the seed of Buddhahood. But if we're caught in the quest for rarity, we forfeit the seed that already lies readily at hand. Dogen's teaching is one of the value of the ordinary, and the truth of the teaching has been shown me repeatedly in my life, but never more so than in the incident involving the sighting of the blue-phase Ross Goose.

ONE WINTER, several of us from the local Audubon group traveled to California's central valley to view waterfowl. We were especially desirous of seeing some Snow Geese and with luck even a few Ross Geese. The trip had produced lots of Snow Geese but not a single Ross Goose when late afternoon brought us to a field of corn stubble being gleaned by a flock of ten to twelve thousand Ross Geese. Now the concept of rarity is postulated on a principle of relative abundance. A few equals "rare." A few more equals "not so rare." So ten thousand or more of anything in one place at one time is a lot and makes for considerable local commonness. Whereas our group had previously been high on the prospects of finding a few Ross Geese, now, confronted with this mob, the initial *oohs* and *aahs* soon subsided into searching the flock for something more stimulating. That's when Alan Baldridge, scanning the flock with a spotting scope, called, "Blue-Phase!"

Now the Blue-Phase of the Ross Goose is fairly rare and many of us had never seen one, so naturally we all wanted to see this rare goose. But the hopes were dismal at best. There were ten thousand of the geese packed into the field and only one among them was the one we now wanted. The desired goose was beyond range of the unassisted eye and, in fact, beyond the capacity of binoculars. Only a spotting scope could give enough magnification to distinguish the blue-phase from among the others. We couldn't expect Alan to give us a peek at the rarity through his scope because the bird was continually moving about among the thousands of others and it was all Alan could do to keep track of it himself. If he lifted his eye from the eyepiece even for a second, the bird would likely be lost to him as well. "Stay with it, Alan," we encouraged him, since Alan's success in tracking the bird was pretty much our only hope of seeing it for ourselves. To add to these difficulties, the sun was rapidly lowering into some patchy clouds, and in the shadowy field the whole flock was beginning to look a little blue.

All of us who had scopes were trying to line up in the general direction of Alan's scope and were scanning the field and, of course, seeing lots of Ross Geese. "How far out is it, Alan? To the front or rear of the flock?" And Alan, with only the discrete image of the blue-phase in his scope, had of course no idea where in the flock the bird was. All he could do was inform us as to whether the blue-phase was moving to his left or right or whatever. On the whole, it was circumstance classic for promoting urgency and frustration. Yet, one by one, some of us were miraculously locating the rarity, so all was not lost.

All was not lost except that an extraordinary old birder among us, Margaret Moody, a woman whose age-enfeebled eyesight had reduced her in this instance to the ordinary, was watching quite another event. She herself had had a lifetime penchant for rarities. In my earliest birding days, when my talent was taxed to identify even the most frequently encountered species, I was given to extolling the virtues of "behavioral observation," trying I suppose to rationalize my own limited capacities and to mask my unmitigated greed for spotting a rarity of my own. "It's not so much what a bird *is*," I explained to Margaret, "but what it *does* that deserves interest." She had simply said, "Oh, I love identifying rarities."

But now the identification of this blue-phase was beyond her reach. Yet she could see well enough to witness how the geese were rising into the sky, thousands at a time, on black-tipped wings that lifted them by some remarkable correspondence avoiding all collision. The strokes of their wings compressing the air overhead washed down on her, past her dim eyes, to call her thoughts into flight. She watched them rise hundreds of feet in great circling sweeps that eventually brought them back to the field where they settled once again. Her binoculars hanging slack about her neck, she watched this. Again and again.

Thankful that the blue-phase wasn't among those who had taken flight, the rest of us were fussing with our scopes and still muttering things like, "Okay, Alan, I think I've got it. Going left over an irrigation ridge, now raising its head." Alan, his eyes watering, his scope image long ago deteriorated to a scratchy blur, would confirm or disconfirm that the action corresponded to that of the bird he was watching.

Later that night at the restaurant, when those of us who had spotted the blue-phase were congratulating ourselves on our good fortune, Margaret never once complained about what she'd missed.

THE QUEST FOR RARITY dulls the palate. Simple tastes become flavorless as one prices one's appetites out of reach of the common market of ordinary goods. The gift of Margaret's weakening eyesight was to return her to the ordinary, where an object or event needn't be novel or exceptional in order to be notable. She was forced to relinquish the rare and exotic. Age had brought her home once again to the interest and beauty of common things. And it wouldn't have to take a flock of ten thousand soaring geese to get her attention, which is after all anything but usual unless you happen to be birding the Pacific flyway. It could be the patches of winter light on the far hillside or the gray winter grass underfoot or the rich odor of dampness drifting off the wetlands. It could be the itchy ride back to the motel with four of us in wet winter woolens packed into the back seat of the car. It could be the string of Yellow-

Headed Blackbirds settling on the barbwire fencing beyond the steamy windshield. It could be the mud stuck to our shoes.

I was bicycling to town the other day and caught a neighbor of mine raking up leaves. I did the required bit about his taking a crack at my leaves when he got through raking his own. He gave the usual retort of telling me he'd love to rake my leaves but didn't want to deprive me of the joy of doing it for myself. When we'd gotten these obligatory exchanges behind us, he told me he'd been looking through some of the fall issues of magazines, and in one of them, he couldn't recall which, he'd seen photographs of the fall colors in the eastern hardwood forests. "Boy that's something," he said. "I'd like to see that. The colors are really something." Well, I'd like to see hardwood forests in autumn myself; still, I couldn't help but notice that both of us were standing in a heap of brilliant red dogwood leaves at the very same time that we were both imagining how beautiful the leaves were elsewhere. And not far down the street was a cascade of golden ginkgo leaves shimmering against a blue sky.

I don't think Dogen's comment that even the coarsest food manifests Buddha nature was meant to suggest that we should never appreciate fine food. I think he was simply warning against disparaging the ordinary by coveting fine food to the exclusion of the coarse. And in the same way, I don't mean to suggest that I should never seek out something special, but only to caution that I not allow the rare beauty of an orchid to dim my delight in the first springing burst of daffodils or distract me from a simple bouquet of yellow daisies or a common sprig of forget-me-not. Of course, Dogen's not talking about literal food alone, but rather the food that feeds the mind. And when a group of birders, eager in their quest for rarity, are rendered indifferent to the spectacle of thousands of white geese repeatedly rising into the air and falling to earth again, they clearly demonstrate a momentary state of mind that has priced itself out of the common beauty of things. And that's the same state of mind that leads any of us to stand in an absolute avalanche of gorgeous fall leaves dreaming of something better.

Beauty

Beauty is truth, truth beauty—that is all
Ye know on earth, and all ye need to know.
—JOHN KEATS

ZEN MASTER LING-YUN, walking a country path one day, rounded the shoulder of a mountain and saw peach blossoms across the way. Peach blossoms would be a common occurrence in the Chinese countryside where he walked in the spring, and yet the sight of them caught him unawares and an unprecedented delight for the beauty of them arose in Ling-yun. It was as if he'd never before seen a peach blossom. Or more accurately, it was as if he'd at once awakened to the sight of the one and only peach blossom that had ever bloomed.

Beauty is like this—single and yet ubiquitous, so that beauty experienced in endlessly unique and variant forms is always one and the same beauty. Other than as form, beauty doesn't manifest at all. Other than its single self, beauty isn't perceived as such.

It's beauty that recognizes beauty. Were the eye of beauty not within us, we would be blind to its appearance. An old saying has it that beauty is in the eye of the beholder, a statement commonly mistakenly to mean that the perception of beauty is merely relative to the circumstances and tastes of the beholder and not inherent in any particular object or event itself. In this sense, the perception of beauty is understood as a wholly arbitrary event in which beauty is nothing in its own right. Yet I feel the truth of this common saying lies in the recognition that while the perception of beauty does in fact reside in the beholder, it's not a perception prejudiced to the beholder's own liking and cannot be willed into effect by any intent on the beholder's part. Like all events, an event of beauty is subject to dependent co-arising: "This being, that becomes; this arising, that arises." Beauty is an arising into being of that sort, touched off in us by the force of beauty that resides within us and over which we exert no direct control.

Another countryside traveler might have passed over Ling-yun's peach blossoms only to be taken up by the patches of sunlight filtering through the branches of trees onto the waters of the valley stream. But this would not mean that the second traveler's indifference to the peach blossoms was evidence that the blossoms manifested no intrinsic beauty, but simply that he discovered his beauty elsewhere. In either instance, each traveler's delight would be in response to the one beauty to be found anywhere.

What Ling-yun saw on the mountain path was a beauty inseparable from his own being—indeed, indistinguishable from his own being. It is said that he was enlightened on the instant. Is then this unrehearsed delight that suddenly seizes us what we mean by enlightenment? Is enlightenment, with all its weighty implications, none other than the perception of beauty? Too simple an explanation perhaps, but the thought of it teases me with a sense of its rightness. That enlightenment is simple has always been apparent to me, so simple in fact that it's almost invariably overlooked long before it's acknowledged. But when at last it gets our attention, enlightenment is always a joyful awakening.

The one who has awakened loves everything she sees, the worst of former appearances shining with a fresh and unexpected beauty. It is said that with enlightenment compassion arises on its own accord. While I would acknowledge the workings of a principled compassion based on a conscious sense of fairness, empathy, and regard toward others, I don't think this is quite what is meant when one refers to the unbidden arising of compassion accompanying the awakening we call enlightenment. What we awaken to is much more a flowering of love than anything else. The loving is the awakening, and it arises as a perception of beauty, so various, so rich, and so unreservedly loved that our world is transformed in an instant.

I don't mean to imply by these remarks that for the enlightened nothing is ever ugly, if ugly is taken to refer to events that are indifferent, harsh, or cruel. Ugliness of this sort is real enough. What I do mean to say is that an event or object doesn't owe its beauty to the relative presence or lack of any other comparable beauty. I don't take delight in a child's laughter relative to the laughter of other children. I don't warm to a smile because a frown is possible. And love is much the same. I don't love something as a result of loving something else less. I simply love the object of my affections for itself and in its own right, without reason or comparison of any sort. This absence of comparative merit is fundamental to the experience of enlightenment. It is an awakening indistinguishable from the arising of beauty with its attendant release of love and joy.

CHRIS, A DEAR FRIEND and Zen student of mine, recently returned from a summer sesshin, a week of silent meditation, to tell me of a great awakening he'd had. He spoke to me of the exact moment when a world previously unseen by him suddenly swam into view. "That was it!" he said, his expression alive with the wonderment of this bright new presence that had opened on his life. And in his telling of it to me, he didn't know whether to laugh or cry, and so did some of both. Chris's account of this moment at the summer sesshin I mark as the first of his ongoing awakenings. It was an awakening that settled like soft delight on everything he saw. And so when he saw Allison, she was beautiful to him. And since he was in love with the world, he loved her too, and before the two of them left the retreat to go their separate ways, he'd chanced to take her by the hand. I mark the moment their hands touched as Chris's second awakening.

After that, with Chris in Chico and Allison in Santa Barbara, the two of them wrote and called each other almost daily, each longing to be together again. And when the chance came, and Chris, waiting at the airport for Allison, saw her there among the other arrivals toss her hair with a little twist of her head the way women sometimes do, he knew she was the love of his life. This, his third awakening, would mark him with the everlasting enlightenment of the beauty and wonder that love is. "Well," you might say, "if falling in love is tantamount to enlightenment, then it's nothing special. Anyone could do it." I would have to agree. It happens all the time.

If I'm looking for beauty, I've already missed it. Its absence is wholly attributable to a failure to observe its presence. The most common way to miss beauty is to hold it to some sort of comparative standard, thus substituting an idea of beauty for the thing itself. I asked Chris once if his love for Allison was relative to his feelings for other women he'd loved. He said that it had never occurred to him to compare her in that way. Other women, or other *lives* for that matter, being whatever they were had nothing to do with Allison.

He loved Allison for herself, and not for any favorable comparison he might attribute to her.

WHILE I MAY RECOGNIZE the presence of beauty, I don't create beauty by that fact, any more than I can be said to create truth, wisdom, or enlightenment by my perception of them. The nature of such insight is one of mutual discovery, awakening to what is already present. As with beauty, it is truth that awakens to truth, wisdom that perceives wisdom, enlightenment that recognizes enlightenment. And always, awakening arrives as a perception of beauty. It flows into the world with an incomparable love that shines on what it sees. It blooms around the bend of whatever path you or I might be walking at this very moment. It flares up in the toss of a woman's hair or the touch of a hand. It raises a question like that of a child's simple inquiry into the nature of things. As with the search for beauty, if I'm looking for an awakening I've already missed it.

Search as long and far as I may, I will not be made wiser or more enlightened than by that which is already given me.

Miracles

THE TERM *MIRACLE* is mostly taken to refer to an event that is extraordinary, something outside normal human experience, a rare occurrence. Yet virtually all human activity, whether of action, speech, or thought, is, in fact, miraculous, and indeed miracles are perfectly commonplace, the most ordinary thing we humans have going for us.

There's a certain quality of religious enthusiasm that wants to enshrine the occult, pointing to seemingly supernatural occurrences as being of particular significance. It's an attitude that has been institutionalized in the Roman Catholic Church's canonization of a saint, where proof of a candidate's performance of one or more miracles is required in order for sainthood to be conferred. And while the Buddha is honored primarily for his teaching and is considered an ordinary human being, there are those who are fascinated by various occult powers sometimes attributed to him. Such a one is often attracted to any event that appears contrary to the laws of nature, and by that consequence regarded as an act of supernatural origin.

If you're fond of miracles, you're in luck, because you're most certainly involved in one at this very moment. I don't need to argue as to whether Jesus walked on water or not, but what about the miracle of his *walking on dry land*? And while he may have fed five thousand hungry pilgrims by the miraculous multiplication of a few scant loaves of bread and a couple fish, yet, by the agency of sun, air, soil, and water, that little miracle of multiplication has been going on for millions of years. And while a Buddhist may be impressed with the unlikely gift of recalling of past lives, what about the equally unlikely gift of this present life? There's nothing here but miracle. It's not something I have to go looking for. Every ordinary thing is ultimately inconceivable.

It's difficult to isolate an example of the inconceivable, considering how everything qualifies. Let's say that I'm playing tennis with a friend and he's just stroked the ball over the net in my direction. What I have to do in order to return the ball is already way beyond anything I can possibly conceive of. There's the direction, trajectory, and speed of the ball to be estimated along with the calculation of the speed and direction of my own body necessary to bring me into position to stroke the ball back over the net. And then there's the stroke itself, the readiness of the arm and wrist, the exact tilt, force, and placement of the racket, the calculation of the distance between me and the net, the height of the net, my opponent's placement, the direction, speed, and trajectory required of a successful return. I'm only partially describing the calculations involved in just one ordinary return of a tennis ball, and yet the extent of that common occurrence that can be done on purpose, that can be conceived of, is infinitesimal in comparison to what has to happen. Every cell in my body, whether of brain, nerve, muscle, or blood, every biochemical exchange, is involved in a simultaneous coordination of such exquisite adjustment that it can only be called miraculous. The workings involved in the stroke of a tennis ball can now be described in nearly infinite scientific detail, but the execution of the living stroke itself remains incomprehensible.

I could just as well cite the miracle of lifting a spoon to my mouth, or the play of my fingers over the keyboard as I write these words, or the choice of words and examples that occur to me as I try to think through the subject at hand, or certainly the process of thinking itself, or whatever brought me to consider this subject in the first place. You see, nothing you or I do can actually be accounted for in some purely conceivable way. The inconceivable is neither distant nor rare nor hidden from sight. It's perfectly visible, right out in the open, occupying your town, neighborhood, and household twenty-four hours a day. It's right under your own roof. I personally can think of nothing that doesn't qualify as miraculous.

And it's not just what we *do* that's inconceivable, it's what we *are* as well. You don't have to look beyond the state of your own being to find a convincing miracle. And you don't have to alter the state of your being to make it more religious or spiritual or enlightened. It's already all of those things.

YEARS AGO WHEN I WAS A STUDENT majoring in English at San Jose State College, a few of us English majors would meet for coffee at the student union. One classmate, a young woman of rather intense seriousness, was forever on the lookout for exceptions to the ordinary, particularly those occasions when she witnessed what she referred to as "an inexplicable conjunction of events." For instance, she might be thinking of her mother just at the moment when her mother called. Or she might be in need of work and happen to apply for a clerical job at a financial institution only to discover among the list of its directors someone bearing her own last name. In her world, these conjunctions were rife with special portent and meaning. She thought of them as spiritual occurrences. She insisted that there was no such thing as coincidence. Nothing happened by chance.

So one afternoon when she and I turned up at the campus library at the same time in search of the same book, she took the occasion to press home the "awesome" dimensions of such a coincidence. She'd read a bit of overblown Buddhist cosmology and took our simultaneous arrival at the library as evidence that she and I shared a deep karmic connection. The fact that the two of us shared an identical class assignment requiring that we consult the one volume of *Medieval Panorama* housed in the campus library didn't seem to discourage her grander speculations. That we shared assignments at all was now seen by her as more than mere coincidence and only served to further persuade her that we'd somehow both been fated to arrive at the library at exactly 2:40 P.M., on a Thursday afternoon.

"What are the odds?" she urged, long aware of my skepticism. "What are the odds of anything?" I answered. "What are the odds of you and I being anywhere at all, whether separately or together," I added. I was thinking of the coincidence of an earth circling a sun or the coincidence of how the walls of the very room in which the two us stood managed somehow to meet the ceiling in perfect conjunction. And what about the simultaneity of heartbeat and coursing blood, or of breath and air? It seemed to me at the moment as if everything fit everything else and that an inexplicable conjunction of events was an ordinary condition of reality. I liked my spiritualist classmate a lot, and had no argument with her sense of the miraculous. It's just that I didn't then and don't now understand why she insisted on limiting the miraculous to a few exceptions. How is it that we human beings fail to see that *everything* is exceptional?

WHAT BUDDHISTS CALL ENLIGHTENMENT is an awakening to the miracle of the ordinary, the immediate perception of all existence as one seamless whole, the inexplicable union of the one in the many, the many in the one. A student of mine came once to tell me about just such an awakening. She wanted to know what it meant. She'd been walking along the banks of Chico Creek, thinking of nothing in particular, her eyes flooded with the whole panorama of creekside valley oaks, sycamores, sky, and water that was spread around her. And then she stopped to rest a bit, settling on the banks of the creek where a pool had formed and a backwater circled slowly round. "I was watching the waters of the creek flow by," she told me, "and then I didn't know who was sitting on the bank watching and who was flowing by. I could feel the current running through me and the place where I circled back on myself. Was that *it*?" she asked.

"It was what it was," I told her.

"Okay," she said, "I'll think of it as the day I traded places with Chico Creek."

"How many places were there to trade?" I asked.

"Two?" she suggested.

"You don't seem convinced," I said.

"One!" she suddenly insisted. "There was one of us!" she said again.

My student didn't know at the time of the classical Buddhist expression of the one in the many embodied in the metaphor of the jeweled net of Indra, which according to legend is a multi-dimensional net comprised of points of multifaceted transparent jewels hung like shining stars in outer space. The image is a metaphor for the universe, in which each jewel receives and returns the reflections of all the other jewels so that every jewel is linked to every other in the whole vast universal net. Each jewel, then, while individual in its own right, is nonetheless so tightly bound up with all the rest that it is indistinguishable from the net itself. Any movement or change in any one of the jewels is a movement and change of the entire net. My student who could not differentiate herself from the flowing stream was unwittingly occupying her place in the jeweled net of Indra, enacting thereby the miracle of the one in the many.

I WAS SENT ONCE BY A KOAN TEACHER to "Count the number of stars in the heavens." I set out to do so, poking my finger at the Milky Way one clear night in an obviously futile effort to tally how many stars were visible. But in the following days, the count went on. I kept coming across stars just about everywhere I looked, a bunch of them hanging in the clothes closet and several calling from the branches of the backyard pistachio tree, a lot more turning up in the kitchen utensil drawer. It wasn't long until my whole world was constructed of stars. I wondered about this and how I could ever get them all counted, until it dawned on me that I was counting the same star repeatedly. All this multiple star stuff was a manifestation of the one and only star. Everything was one existence, in the same way in which multitudinous sea waves in all their discrete particularity are one ocean. It is this basic, overarching, omnipresent miracle of the one out of which all the "many" miracles of person, object, and event arise. The miraculous is ubiquitous.

One reason this common miracle so often goes unnoticed is due to the way perception occurs. The Buddha taught that consciousness is always consciousness of something in particular. There's no such thing as an unengaged consciousness waiting around to be conscious of something. Consciousness co-arises with the juxtaposition of a sense organ and sense object. When I see something, sight consciousness occurs, and so on for the other senses. The way that perception occurs is for one or more of our senses to draw an object out of the background into the foreground, where, by means of a necessarily limiting focus, the foreground object constitutes our perception and becomes momentarily exceptional to all the rest. The significance of the background correspondingly fades for the instant in relationship to that of the foreground figure.

Not only that, but it is the nature of our senses that we can draw but one figure at a time out of the background into the foreground, so that the foreground figure thus singled out constitutes the entirety of the present experience. It may seem as though we're getting the broad picture all at once—the frog on the rock as well as the berry vines beyond and the nearby man walking his dog—but this impression is only because the point of focus shifts consecutively from one object to another in the tiniest fraction of an instant. But the actual sense perception of more than one object is never simultaneous. This limit constitutes a failure to generalize and is like singling out one particular jewel in the net of Indra and failing to recognize its relationship with the whole net.

But while it's beyond the capacity of sense perception to generalize, mind itself, through the agency of memory, *is* capable of generalizing, and can perceive the background out of which an object or event rises to consciousness. Mind comprehends the foreground and background as one inseparable whole. It realizes the context in which things occur, the space in which persons, objects, and events play out their lives as one instrument of being. Mind is at once the river flowing and the watcher on the bank, both sense and sense object, perceiver and the perceived, knower and the known.

In the room where I write is a plain wooden chair with a slatted seat and back. If I glance in the chair's direction, it will likely swim into focus and for the moment seem ordinary. But if I call into being mind's awareness of the chair's context, of the space it occupies not only within the room but under the arching sky itself within a curved and limitless universe, then the chair is inconceivable. As is the paper clip on the desktop or the keyboard with which I'm typing. Should I happen to be looking for a miracle, I've got it right here under my fingertips.

Incense

AT HIGH DESERT STATE PRISON where I serve as Buddhist chaplain, the Buddhist inmates are always clamoring for incense. In accord with California Department of Corrections regulations, I'm not supposed to give them any (under threat of permanent expulsion from the prison)—and so I've had to refuse to do so.

To understand why the refusal pains me so, you need to understand how the prisoners live and what a stick of incense apparently means to them. I only had to visit the compound once to see how they lived, though the deepening realization of what such a life was like took time to seep into my imagination. But I was longer in understanding why they so badly wanted incense to burn. As a Buddhist, I've participated in ritual behaviors for years and should have understood earlier. But let me begin with what the daily life of an inmate at the prison is like.

AN INMATE AT HIGH DESERT STATE PRISON is housed in a cell six feet wide by nine feet long, fifty-four square feet of floor space in all. These cells were initially designed to house a single prisoner. But in C-yard, which holds the largest contingent of Buddhist inmates, two prisoners are crammed into the same space. By the time you deduct the space occupied by the standard complement of bunk beds, a writing table, a straight chair, two wall hung shelves, and a toilet and wash basin, neither inmate can traverse the length of the cell without the other crawling onto the bed to let him by.

Not only that, but the cells are the most oppressively isolating cubicles one can imagine. The floor, walls, and ceiling of the cells are solid, unadorned concrete, relieved only by two tiny slit windows. One of the windows faces inward toward the interior of the building where an armed guard on an elevated platform electronically controls the solid steel doors that open and close the cells. From inside the cell, the guard, pacing back and forth in his green uniform with a high-caliber rifle slung over his shoulder, is the only human being other than his cellmate that an inmate is able to see. The other window looks out the back of the cell on an empty patch of dirt and a blank wall. It's like being housed in a crypt. Most of the inmates at High Desert State Prison are serving life sentences and may very well spend the entirety of their lives in such isolating confinement.

This would be bad enough if the cells served primarily as bedrooms and the inmates only slept here, but on the best of days they are released into the exercise yard for four hours at the most, leaving the other twenty hours to be endured inside these concrete boxes. But even worse, when the yard is "locked down," the inmates are restricted to their cells for twenty-three-and-a-half hours a day and allowed only a half-hour's trip to the shower cell.

When I first came to C-yard as a chaplain, the inmates were locked down—and had been for more than two years. I walked about on the catwalks and knocked on cell doors. A face would appear in the narrow vertical slit of the window, and we would look at each other through the heavy reinforced glass. We had to more or less shout at each other in order for the sound of our voices to penetrate the thickness of the barrier that separated us.

Since inmates that are locked down aren't allowed to attend group meetings, it was by way of these cell-by-cell visitations that I began my teaching in C-yard. I taught zazen, and one day when I asked an inmate if he'd been doing his daily sitting, he bowed and drew away from the window. I watched him remove his blankets from the lower bunk where he slept. He folded them into a little stack of about four inches high and laid them on the bare concrete floor right up against the seatless and lidless stainless steel toilet, which happened to be the one place in the room where there was floor space enough to sit cross legged. And then he sat down to show me that he'd been doing what I'd taught him to do. I watched him there on his little stack of blankets with his bony legs and feet pressed against the cold concrete, so proud to show me how he'd worked it all out. "If I had some incense," he told me later, "I could do it right."

I turned away his request, telling him that I wasn't allowed to bring him any items for his personal use. But I was troubled by the degree to which the guards hold all the controls at High Desert State Prison while the inmates are purposely and systematically rendered powerless. This young Buddhist, like all the inmates at the prison, was deprived of the slightest thing he might want to do on his own. Still, he'd been able to stack his blankets at will and sit on the cell floor and do zazen without having to get permission or be told he wasn't allowed to do so. And apparently this meant a lot to him, though he thought he could do it better if he just had some incense to burn.

When C-yard was eventually unlocked and the inmates were at last allowed out of their cells to attend Buddhist services, sixty inmates showed up for zazen and instruction. Under heavy guard, they lined up outside the C-yard chapel door where they were body-searched one at a time and let in to meet with me. For the first time, I occupied the same space with them, without an impenetrable steel door separating us. I could talk to them at last without shouting through a narrow band of thick glass. To tell the truth, I felt a little shy in this unrestricted proximity. Things went along well enough, the number of attendees gradually settling down to a serious and dedicated forty inmates. They took turns lighting incense at the chapel services, a ritual they were anxious to perform. But they never let up on wanting incense to take back to their cells. "Couldn't you just bring some to service and hand it out?" they urged.

I looked into this, checking once again the regulations that applied and found a curious contradiction. While the injunction against delivering personal gifts to any single inmate was unequivocal, the regulations did allow for certain religious items to be distributed *en masse* where no distinction was made between individuals. This meant that I could hand out items to the group as a whole, so long as they were all treated equally. And then on an entirely separate page featuring the religious artifacts inmates were allowed to have, I found incense listed. But, then again, primary among items listed as forbidden to inmates was anything with which a stick of incense could be lit.

The next time I was questioned about it, I told the inmate, "I could bring you incense, but you wouldn't have any way to light it." He grinned at me. "What?" I asked. "I can get it lit," was all he said. It wasn't until later that I learned how this was done by inserting two paper clips (also forbidden contraband) into an electrical socket and arcing it. Why would anything so seemingly inconsequential as a stick of incense bring one to risk electrocution at the most, or at the least, eventual detection and punishment by the guards?

I can find an answer to my own question no further away than the reach of my arm, where an heirloom teacup and saucer rest on a tabletop. It's my custom to drink tea or coffee from a proper cup and saucer, and I've done so for most of my adult life. I feel deprived when forced to drink from a mug. At meals, I set out cloth napkins, never paper. I begin each day with a period of zazen, striking the gong three times for the start, never two nor one. My life is admittedly embedded with ritual behaviors both traditional and of my own introduction. I have a host of such "inconsequential" familiarities that would leave me distressed in their absence. For the inmates at High Desert State Prison, *every* familiarity of their former life is absent. It's not hard for me to understand how they might think it worth putting themselves at risk for a stick of incense.

I'm aware of the admonition against attachment to form, wherein too strong a concern for ritual is seen as a distraction from the true essence of Zen practice. But Zen practice has always been wholly inclusive for me, and I simply can't imagine anything I might do, ritualistic or not, as being anything other than Zen practice. After all, zazen itself, which is the foundation of Buddhist practice, is pretty formal and certainly as ritualistic as lighting incense or ringing gongs or even bowing for that matter. At any rate I can't imagine myself cautioning the prison inmates against the use of incense on the basis of exercising non-attachment to form. They want it too badly for me to trouble them with distinctions of that kind. Personally, I wouldn't care if they lit incense all day and night, mumbling prayers and Amitabha chants with each new stick, if it would help them feel less isolated and hopeless and give them one cultural familiarity to indulge. Besides, while attachment to form might well be a hindrance to realizing the essential essence of Zen practice, it's also true that Zen practice, essential or otherwise, manifests solely and exclusively as form. Lighting a stick of incense will do as well for a Zen practice as will anything else—certainly as well, in this case, as hearing a Dharma talk on non-attachment.

I DEARLY WISH I could tell you that I distributed incense to the Buddhist inmates, but on the very eve of doing so, revised regulations were given out naming incense among other contraband items forbidden in the prison. So by a government agency beyond our influence and control, the issue has been resolved for the inmates and me. But beneath my own ribs and dearer to the heart than I had imagined, I feel the pulse of those ancient ritual enactments that give common shape to our strange and disparate lives. My prison students have taught me once more how much I depend on the comforting objects and rituals that support the days and hours of my life. If together the students and I can acknowledge the role of ritual in our lives with forbearance and mutual understanding, perhaps we will come in time to let go of the need of such things more easily than we do now.

Helping

A STORY IS TOLD that one day Layman P'ang and his daughter Ling-chao were out selling baskets. They were just coming down off a bridge when Layman P'ang stumbled and fell to the ground. Ling-chao immediately threw herself down alongside him. Layman P'ang, taken by surprise, said, "What are you doing?" "I saw you fall to the ground, Father," she said, "and so I'm helping." Layman P'ang laughed, and said, "Fortunately, no one was looking."

But of course the story has been told and retold through the centuries and now many of us are looking. Maybe Ling-chao's response wasn't as foolish as it might seem. And maybe Layman P'ang recognized the aptness of his daughter's peculiar offering of help. If so, how was it apt, and what sort of help could such a response be said to offer?

The most notable difference between Ling-chao's response and the more likely response of helping the fallen father back to his feet is that Ling-chao wasn't trying to change her father's situation, but chose instead to go along with his fall. A student once complained to me of her "bad temper." "I get angry too much," she told me. "I need to control my anger." "Maybe you're not angry enough," I said, taking sides with her anger in a movement like that of Ling-chao throwing herself down beside her father. My student felt victimized by anger as though it were an unfortunate disposition she'd inherited like the length of her fingers or hair color. I wanted her to see that anger was something she was doing on her own accord. If she could join forces with her anger, she might discover the degree to which she herself promotes these unwanted bouts of ill temper. And with that discovery, she could take back the power of choice she'd otherwise forfeited to forces she'd mistakenly assumed to lie beyond her control. I was asking her to fall to the ground on purpose. "If you're going to do it, do it right," I said. "And if you're not sure how it's done, give it a little help. It's *your* anger after all."

Others may fare differently, but it works best for me when I can manage to go along with rather than resist unwanted feelings. Besides, I've never been successful in *not* having a feeling I was, in fact, having. But by "going along with" a feeling, I don't mean necessarily *indulging* the feeling by acting on it or weaving a self-justifying story regarding its nature. But it helps to bed down with whatever feeling or mood I'm resisting and acquaint myself with the nature of its appeal for me. If I'm curious and respectful of a feeling, I might find out what part I'm playing in its origination. So if I'm angry, as my student complained of being, I don't choose to vent my anger on others, but I don't deny the anger its full right of existence either. That way I have a chance to discover how it serves me and why I hang on to it as I do. The same is true of other unwanted feelings—chronic jealousy, fear, melancholy, and greed, a persistent grief that refuses consolation, and so forth. My own doing augments these common states of suffering when they occur, and it's helpful to discover why I do them.

It's a characteristic of human behavior that when we come upon someone in distress, we're often moved to help and comfort the person somehow. This natural response to another's suffering is what we call *compassion*. The etymological roots of *compassion* reveal the term to mean something like "suffering with." So compassion is understood to be as much a matter of sharing or joining someone in his distress as it is about alleviating the distress. Besides, I'm not sure that it's ever possible to actually lift the weight of another's suffering from his shoulders, but it is sometimes possible to keep him company until he feels better. "Suffering with" is counter to trying to fix the suffering, which, if the suffering is self-originated, can only be fixed by the sufferer himself, and can't be fixed at all if the suffering, like death or injury, is unavoidable.

Sometimes when someone you love suffers, "suffering with" is the only option available, and when that happens it can be a great teaching for the helping heart.

WHEN I WAS A BOY, two of my parent's best friends were Carla and George Wanger. They had a little girl whom they named Rita and who seemed normal as an infant, developing far enough to crawl about a little on hands and knees. But she never walked nor spoke and in time was unable even to lift her own head from a pillow. Yet, remarkably, she lived for fourteen years and grew to a length of over five feet. The Wangers set up a hospital bed in their living room so as to be near her when needed. The child, Rita, and then later the girl, Rita, unable at the last to command even the least movement of an arm or leg, wasted silently away, year after year, a skeleton clothed in a shroud of loose skin. I sometimes watched her in her suffering, peering up at her on the high bed, and though she was absolutely mute, I was convinced even as a child that she knew what was happening to her.

When Rita was distressed, she had a way of telegraphing her suffering to others in the room, a kind of subtle motion that rolled through her bony frame, a play of pain about her mouth, a sharpness of breath, and if you looked closely sometimes silent tears would leak from her eyes. She would ask for help in these ways, and Carla, who was particularly sensitive to these appeals, knew, even in the darkened nighttime room that her child needed her. Carla would slip into bed alongside Rita and, lying on her back, pull the child up onto her own body, stretching her out full length and face down from head to foot. And there they lay, Rita's bony frame draped over her mother's softer flesh. Nothing else ever quieted the child, and in time Rita's breathing would slow and she'd fall asleep and Carla would roll her back on the mattress and tuck her in.

What must it have been like to literally draw your daughter's grief up over your body like a blanket of sorrow, her heart beating against yours, her every breath drawn into your own lungs, lying there in utter surrender to the child's suffering? Rita died this way one night, draped over the soft warmth of her mother's body. Some things can't be fixed, and knowing that, Carla had chosen to join her daughter in the child's long journey toward death, answering death's ultimate dictum with a mother's durable love. In the morning, Carla washed Rita's body and dressed her in a fresh gown, inviting those of us who'd known Rita to come and say goodbye to her before the undertakers took her away. Carla had not asked that things be other than they were, yielding to necessary circumstance. "I see you have fallen, child; let me join you in your fall."

MOST OF US have joined in the fall of others—times of injury, disease, death, and loss, things that can't be made otherwise. But not all life's intractable consequences are of such gravity. When my son, Dru, was just entering his senior year at high school, he was assigned a seat in Senior English alongside a classmate, Kay, and the two of them were soon caught up in the sharp intensity of their first love.

The relationship lasted for over a year, the two of them walking in the woods, singing songs together in the upstairs bedroom to the accompaniment of Dru's guitar, asking for the Scrabble set once so that they might play a game. But there came a time when I arrived home from work to find my son piteously heartbroken and weeping. Kay had decided to break off the relationship. I'd once had just such a first love myself, and I knew the heartbreak my son was undergoing. But I didn't tell him that the pain would eventually pass and that time would heal the hurt. Instead I held him while he shook, knowing that love's own wounded outcry would mend him in ways no consolation of mine ever could. Later, Dru played the guitar and I sang, recording our own version of a Bob Dylan song.

OF COURSE NOT ALL SUFFERING benefits from being accommodated. I've known addiction and wouldn't want to accommodate an alcohol or drug addict, encouraging him to go along with "his abuse." Instead I'd intervene because until the addict dries out he's unable to inquire into the roots of his suffering. He must stop what he's doing before he can assess his need for doing it. There are forms of violence and cruelty that are also like this and must be stopped before any rehabilitation is possible. Sometimes "No!" is the only appropriate help to be given. Once the momentum of habit is stalled, the underlying pain will surface. Only then will the suffering be laid open to the sufferer's full acquaintance, stripped of its power of persuasion and put to rest.

LONG AGO a daughter threw herself headlong onto the ground in a seemingly absurd gesture of helping her fallen father. I don't know whether she thought about what she was doing or just did it out of some inexplicable urging of her body and mind. But in joining herself as she did to her father's predicament, she registered throughout time a compassionate wisdom that serves me even now. In my mind's eye, I sometimes see myself lying where she once lay.

And I say to whomever suffers, "Do you hurt? Let me help you with that."

How the Mind Returns

IN THE *TENZO KYOKAN*, ZEN Master Dogen writes, "You should practice in such a way that things come and abide in your mind, and your mind returns and abides in things, all through the day and night." That things come and abide in my mind seems to me a matter of receptive awareness that's quite different from a mind that goes out after things. At heart, it's an exposure accompanying an uncalculated sincerity. It's not concentration or intentional observation of any sort but is rather an innocent mindfulness in which things take residence in my mind. They come upon me without notice, arriving as unanticipated guests all through the day and night like shadows sliding onto the moon or like morning dew drifting among the trees, moistening my face and hair. Things sometimes enter by way of sight like forked lightning against a blue-black sky, or enter by way of sound like the wail of a siren or squirrels squeaking in the branches overhead. If things are to come and abide in my mind, all that's asked of me is that I be present. What Buddhists call mindfulness is, for me, an unprepared and neutral mind like that of a mirror in which a reflection of the world appears.

But the practice of mindfulness is not by itself wisdom. Dogen teaches that not only should I practice so that things come and abide in my mind but my mind must return and abide in things as well. Wisdom is a willingness to both receive and return. And to effect this return requires that I be alive in all things as all things are alive in me.

Shunryu Suzuki tells this story of Dogen: Whenever Dogen dipped water from the river at Eiheiji monastery, he used only half a dipperful and returned the other half to the river. Suzuki says that this practice of Dogen's was "not based on any idea of being economical." For Suzuki, the return of half the water was an intuitive response resulting from feeling at one with the river. And then Suzuki touches upon the great wisdom of the mind's return to abide in things, saying, "When we dip part of the river into a dipper, we experience some feeling of the water, and we also feel the value of the person who uses the water. Feeling ourselves and the water in this way, we cannot use it in just a material way. It is a living thing."

And what is *not* a living thing? What could possibly be excluded? Surely the grassy bank where Dogen knelt to draw water is equally alive, and the stones lining the river bottom, and the sandals on Dogen's feet, and the dipper itself. I like to imagine that with the dipperful of water drawn up by Dogen the river came to abide in his mind, and in the return of a half dipperful of water, Dogen's mind went to abide in the river, so that the river's mind and Dogen's mind were one. It is a return that closes the circle between mind and matter where all perceptions are reciprocal. I cannot see the sycamore on the banks of Chico Creek without being seen by it as well. Everywhere I look, I peer into a reflection of my own likeness. I flow with the river to the sea and return again to the mountaintop.

I'm always coming back, making my return like a planet in orbit round its star. The mind that returns to abide in things is naturally and necessarily inclusive.

Karen and I abide in each other as necessarily as breath abides in life. If I'm having friends in for a holiday and I ask Brad to come, I'll ask his friend, David, as well, and Pam and Mary-Michael. These friends and I cannot help but abide in each other just as mountains abide in the plains or as continents cradle oceans. With all our apparent differences, we are yet as acorns scattered beneath a single parent tree, and cannot but acknowledge our common heritage. The presence of my friends takes up my mind in this way. It is this expanding inclusiveness that constitutes the mind's return to itself. I am what I include and nothing's left outside.

The mind makes its intuitive return in ordinary and practical ways—greetings returned for greetings, smiles for smiles, laughter for a well-told joke, comfort for another's sorrow. I can return kitchen waste to the soil, save leftovers for another meal, recycle and reuse whatever I can. I can return the delight of morning sunlight to the place of its rising there on the eastern mountains. I can give back the joy I feel in a sparrow's song.

Zazen

A ZEN BUDDHIST'S LIFE is as active as anyone's. Yet we meditators view the world as much from the horizontal as from the vertical, where we engage life at the approximate level of the floor, cross-legged, alert, watchful, and unmoving. We call this stationary mode of travel *zazen*.

Every roof, every household, needs the support of a foundation. For the Zen Buddhist the foundation of the Buddha's house is zazen. It's a practice that teaches me to stay put in my own life wherever circumstance happens to find me at the moment, trusting that the roof and walls have their own support and won't collapse on me. Zazen makes a home of everywhere. If I am brought to some sort of peace and calm by zazen, it's precisely because I have settled into my actual life.

IN KOSHO UCHIYAMA'S CLASSIC WORK, *Opening the Hand of Thought*, he points out that Buddhism is a religion without a god, and asks, "What then is the basis for peace of mind?" Answering his own question, Uchiyama says, "In Buddhism the fundamental posture in contrast to bowing down before god is zazen." He calls zazen the practice of "the self settling into the true and immovable self." It is when I quit looking elsewhere and allow the self to settle in itself that I discover that with all my faults I'm nonetheless "imperfectly" whole and adequate as I am, and that there's no need to go looking elsewhere. As Uchiyama says, "From the time Shakyamuni Buddha taught that the self must settle into itself, truly and firmly, this teaching has been the principal attitude of Buddhism." I would only add that such a settling is not an attitude but a deeply felt reality that constitutes the only true refuge.

I may find it disappointing and be wary of the contention that I'm my own refuge, a household unto myself. But if I insist on seeking sanctuary outside my present being and circumstance, grasping at those enticing conceptualizations of Buddha Nature, enlightenment, God, salvation, Heaven, nirvana, and such, I'll only end up constructing a refuge of nothing more than my own wishful thinking. The truth is emptier than that and is encountered on the cushion. Zazen, the self settling in itself, can't be encompassed by any wishful thought of mine. It's the living pulse of my own being that has nowhere it needs to go and is always at home. Zazen awakens me to the present wonder of being human, and welcomes me into the Buddha's universal household.

Housekeeping: An Epilogue

OUSEKEEPING IN THE BUDDHA'S HOUSEHOLD is thorough and leaves nothing out. It's a matter of bringing everything home, or as Chögyam Trungpa Rinpoche puts it, "Carry whatever occurs in life onto the path." If I make distinctions between what's significant and what's not, I can't get the work properly done, and whatever housework I mistakenly consider unimportant will be hours of labor unnecessarily wasted.

But in the Buddha's household nothing's unimportant; in the Buddha's household everything matters equally. I'm only able to keep the household in order when I can mash potatoes or carry out the trash or turn the compost heap with the same care I would give to speaking before the city council or leading a Zen retreat or writing a Dharma book such as this. If people ask me how my Zen practice is going, they might as well be asking me how my life is going because I can't discover a valid distinction between the two. That's why I don't particularly like the word "spiritual," which in popular usage sets up a distinction between what's spiritual and what's not. Is chanting the Heart Sutra more or less spiritual, more or less a matter of Zen practice, than driving your daughter to school or helping clean up after dinner?

So you see, the Buddha's household happens to be wherever I am at the moment, and the Buddha's housekeeping is whatever I'm doing at the moment. Should I happen to travel to India or Africa, I will not have noticeably left home. Buddha's housekeeping is a frame of mind, an attention given equally to whatever occurs, a generous reception granted to whatever the world offers.

In my particular case, the world has recently offered me a cat. It wanders in and out of my backyard, a rather large, gray and brown Siamese. It's a little cautious of me, but mostly undisturbed and apparently unimpressed as well by my presence. Once in a while its almond-shaped blue eyes will engage me in such a way as to confirm that we've agreed to let one another be.

I have a garden Buddha in the backyard, set against a mossy wall between a fern and a rhododendron plant, and it so happened that the other day I came upon the cat perched alongside the Buddha, between it and the rhododendron. It was wetting its paws and washing its face the way cats do. I know it saw me, but it studiously appeared not to (also the way cats do), but it eventually quit washing and sat perfectly still and upright next to the meditating Buddha, as though to challenge me to any distinction I might want to make between the two.

If I'd had an inclination to bow, and in truth I did have a bit of an inclination to do so, I wouldn't know which Buddha to bow to—the plaster Buddha or the one with fur. It's a moot question, though, because in the Buddha's household you can't bow to just one thing. If I bow to the cat, I've bowed to the fern, the rhododendron, the mossy wall, and the statue of the Buddha as well. It wouldn't change circumstances any if I went back into the house and bowed to the kitchen cabinets. Everything I bow to in the whole of the Buddha's vast household is bowing to Buddha, and in fact I *do* bow to the kitchen cabinets, pots and pans, serving spoons, the refrigerator, onions, carrots, beets, beans, potatoes—you name it. If it's found in a kitchen, I probably have indeed bowed to it. That's how the Buddha's housekeeping is done.

ZEN MASTER DOGEN understood the household situation better than anyone I know of. He wrote what I think of as my kitchen-training manual. The first Buddhist literature I ever read was the *Tenzo Kyokan*, Dogen's "instructions to the cook." I generally cook the evening meals for Karen and me, and for guests when we have them in, and the kitchen is a kind of proving ground for my life as a whole. Dogen taught me to be at home in the kitchen and make peace with what I found there:

> The Chief Cook must not eye the food superficially or with a discriminatory mind; his mind must be so free that the Buddha Land appears within a blade of grass, whenever he or others behold it, and he must be capable of giving a great sermon even on the heart of a particle of dust. He must not be contemptuous when making poor-quality soup, nor should he be overjoyed when he makes it with milk; if he is unattached to the last, he will not dislike the first.

When Dogen cautions against the discriminatory mind, he doesn't mean that I should make no distinction between thyme and oregano or salt and pepper, or that I should be oblivious to how much onion to add to a dish or whether to bake it covered or uncovered and at what temperature. What he means is that I should not disparage, even to myself, one food over another, so that however meager or plain or tough or flavorless a food might be, I treat it with the greatest possible regard and make of it the best I can. It is *preferential* discrimination that leads one's cooking and one's life astray.

Dogen cautions as well against moral discrimination:

> It would be thoroughly wicked of [the chief cook] to judge others by his own standards; all members of the Sangha are the treasure of Buddhism, whether senior or junior, clever or stupid—that which was wrong yesterday may be correct today; it is impossible to separate the sacred from the secular. . . . One must be entirely free from moral discrimination. A mind of utter sincerity, free from preference, is the True Way.

Well, the wickedness lies in a standard of moral preference that admits some and excludes others. And it doesn't matter what defense I'm prepared to offer in service of my particular moral discrimination, because my "truth," whatever it might happen to be, is not the truth of Dogen's "true way." The true way is purely a matter of housekeeping, and in the house of the Buddha, one room or one activity is not better or worse than another. And neither is one person. All is met equally, which is the very meaning of Dogen's mind of sincerity. I take up residence in the Buddha's household when I give myself wholeheartedly to whatever I'm doing, wherever I'm doing it, and whomever I happen to meet there.

Index

About the Author

L IN JENSEN IS THE AUTHOR OF *Pavement,* which chronicled his experiences as a protester for peace, and *Bad Dog!,* a *Shambhala Sun* "Best Buddhist Writing" selection. He is the founding teacher and senior teacher emeritus of the Chico Zen Sangha, in Chico, California, where he lives with his wife.

About Wisdom Publications

WISDOM PUBLICATIONS, a nonprofit publisher, is dedicated to making available authentic works relating to Buddhism for the benefit of all. We publish books by ancient and modern masters in all traditions of Buddhism, translations of important texts, and original scholarship. Additionally, we offer books that explore East-West themes unfolding as traditional Buddhism encounters our modern culture in all its aspects. Our titles are published with the appreciation of Buddhism as a living philosophy, and with the special commitment to preserve and transmit important works from Buddhism's many traditions.

To learn more about Wisdom, or to browse books online, visit our website at www.wisdompubs.org.

You may request a copy of our catalog online or by writing to this address:

Wisdom Publications
199 Elm Street
Somerville, Massachusetts 02144 USA
Telephone: 617-776-7416
Fax: 617-776-7841
Email: info@wisdompubs.org
www.wisdompubs.org

THE WISDOM TRUST

As a nonprofit publisher, Wisdom is dedicated to the publication of Dharma books for the benefit of all sentient beings and dependent upon the kindness and generosity of sponsors in order to do so. If you would like to make a donation to Wisdom, you may do so through our website or our Somerville office. If you would like to help sponsor the publication of a book, please write or email us at the address above.

Thank you.

Wisdom is a nonprofit, charitable 501(c)(3) organization affiliated with the Foundation for the Preservation of the Mahayana Tradition (FPMT).

Also available from Wisdom Publications

Bad Dog!
A Memoir of Love, Beauty, and Redemption in Dark Places
Lin Jensen
288 pages | ISBN 0861714865 | $15.95

Bad Dog! is a vivid testament to the unforeseen love, beauty, and redemption discovered in the most difficult times and places. *Bad Dog!* reads like a collection of closely linked short stories but is in fact a work of literary nonfiction. *Bad Dog!* will appeal to anyone who has fallen into dark places and wants to climb back into the light.

Pavement
Reflections on Mercy, Activism, and Doing "Nothing" for Peace
Lin Jensen
144 pages | ISBN 0861715225 | $12.95

There's a war on—and Lin Jensen isn't gonna take it standing up. In thirty-six riveting scenes, *Pavement* shows how the Buddhist perspective can help us all, even in the toughest times. Every day, Lin Jensen went down to the center of his small town of Chico, California, plopped down a meditation cushion, and sat "peace vigils" in protest of the US invasion of Iraq. *Pavement* is the story of his honest effort to change the world.